"Nolo's home page is worth bookmarking."
—WALL STREET JOURNAL

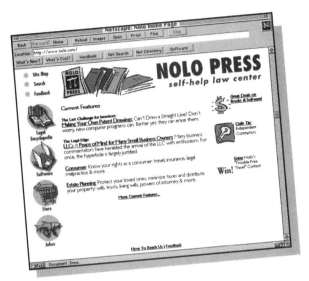

LEGAL INFORMATION ONLINE

www.nolo.com

24 hours a day

AT THE NOLO PRESS SELF-HELP LAW CENTER ON THE WEB, YOU'LL FIND

- Nolo's comprehensive Legal Encyclopedia, with links to other online resources
- Downloadable demos of Nolo software and sample chapters of many Nolo books
- An online law store with a secure online ordering system
- Our ever-popular lawyer jokes
- Discounts and other good deals, our hilarious Shark Talk game

THE NOLO NEWS

Stay on top of important legal changes with Nolo's quarterly magazine, *The Nolo News*. Start your free one-year subscription by filling out and mailing the response card in the back of this book. With each issue, you'll get legal news about topics that affect you every day, reviews of legal books by other publishers, the latest Nolo catalog, scintillating advice from Auntie Nolo and a fresh batch of our famous lawyer jokes.

S0-BOT-377

LEASEWRITER™

Users' Guide
by Ely Newman

■

a special LEASEWRITER edition of

Leases & Rental Agreements

by Marcia Stewart and Attorneys
Janet Portman and Ralph Warner

NOLO PRESS  BERKELEY

Your Responsibility When Using Self-Help Law Books & Software

We've done our best to give you useful and accurate information in this software. But laws and procedures change frequently and are subject to differing interpretations. If you want legal advice backed by a guarantee, see a lawyer. If you use this software, it's your responsibility to make sure that the facts and general advice contained in it apply to your situation.

Keeping Up-to-Date

To keep its books and software up to date, Nolo Press issues new printings and new editions periodically. New printings reflect minor legal changes and technical corrections. New editions contain major legal changes, major text additions or major reorganizations. To find out if a later printing or edition of any Nolo book is available, call Nolo Press at 510-549-1976 or check the catalog in the *Nolo News*, our quarterly publication. You can also contact us on the Internet at www.nolo.com.

To stay current, follow the "Update" service in the *Nolo News*. You can get a free one-year subscription by sending us the registration card included in your *LeaseWriter* package.

1st Edition	**OCTOBER 1998**
Conceptual Design	Albin Renauer, Jenya Chernoff & Karen Turk
Software Development	Albin Renauer, Jenya Chernoff, Karen Turk, Allen Santos, Jimmy Leung
Editorial	Marcia Stewart
Documentation	Ely Newman
Production	Susan Putney
Box/Cover design	Linda M. Wanczyk
Proofreading	Robert Wells
Index	Jane Meyerhofer
Printing	Bertelsmann Industry Services

Stewart, Marcia.

    LeaseWriter : by Marcia Stewart, Ralph Warner, Janet Portman
       p. cm.
    Includes index.
    ISBN 0-87337-413-4
    1. Leases--United States--Popular works. 2. Leases--United
    States--Forms. 3. Leases--United States--Automation. I. Warner,
    Ralph E. II. Portman, Janet. III. Title.
    KF590.Z9S746 1998
    346.7304'346--dc21   98-16691
                                              CIP

Acknowledgments

LeaseWriter is the result of the creative and hard work of many Nolo people. Special thanks to:

Albin Renauer for knowing it could be done and overall mentoring

Jenya Chernoff, Albin Renauer and Karen Turk for project design and endless scriptwriting

Marcia Stewart for writing the Legal Help and overall editing support

Jenya Chernoff for her imaginative graphics

Ely Newman for the users' guide and a thousand good ideas

Jimmy Leung, bug-finder par excellence, for all his indispensable help

Allen Santos and Cathy Neuren for testing

Linda Wanczyk and Erin Douglas for the terrific box design and copy

Susan Putney for laying out the manual and making the production process go so smoothly

Stan Jacobsen for research assistance

Sheryl Rose for proofreading, and

Natalie DeJarlais for chocolate.

Finally, an extra special thanks to Nolo publisher Jake Warner. *LeaseWriter* would never have been done without Jake's interest and encouragement.

This is a software license agreement between Nolo Press and you as purchaser, for the use of the *LeaseWriter* program and accompanying manual. By using this program and manual, you indicate that you accept all terms of this agreement. If you do not agree to all the terms and conditions of this agreement, do not use the *LeaseWriter* program or manual, but return both to Nolo Press for a full refund.

Grant of License

In consideration of payment of the license fee, which is part of the price you paid for *LeaseWriter*, Nolo Press as licensor grants to you the right to use the enclosed program to produce wills for yourself and your immediate family, subject to the terms and restrictions set forth in this license agreement.

Copy, Use and Transfer Restrictions

The *LeaseWriter* manual and the program and its documentation are copyrighted. You may not give, sell or otherwise distribute copies of the program to third parties, except as provided in the U.S. Copyright Act. Under this license agreement, you may not use the program for commercial or nonprofit purposes, or use the program to prepare documents for people outside your immediate family.

Commercial Use of This Product

For information regarding commercial licensing of this product, including use by educational institutions and nonprofit organizations, call Nolo Press at 510-549-1976.

Disclaimer of Warranty and Limited Warranty

This program and accompanying manual are sold "AS IS," without any implied or express warranty as to their performance or to the results that may be obtained by using the program.

As to the original purchaser only, Nolo Press warrants that the magnetic disk on which the program is recorded shall be free from defects in material and workmanship in normal use and service. If a defect in this disk occurs, the disk may be returned to Nolo Press. We will replace the disk free of charge. In the event of a defect, your exclusive remedy is expressly limited to replacement of the disk as described above.

Your Responsibilities for Your Documents

Although best efforts were devoted to making this material useful, accurate and up to date, please be aware that state laws and procedures change and may be interpreted differently. Also, we have no control over whether you carefully follow our instructions or properly understand the information in the *LeaseWriter* software or manual.

Of necessity, therefore, Nolo Press does not make any guarantees about the use to which the software or manual are put, or the results of that use.

Term

The license is in effect until terminated. You may terminate it at any time by destroying the program together with all copies and modifications in any form.

Entire Agreement

By using the *LeaseWriter* program, you agree that this license is the complete and exclusive statement of the agreement between you and Nolo Press regarding *LeaseWriter*.

About Nolo Press

The leading publisher of self-help law books and software since 1971

Nolo Press was founded in 1971 to show people how to do their own routine legal tasks and avoid costly lawyer fees. Early on, bar associations thundered against self-help law, claiming that lawyers were essential to help with even simple legal procedures. But Nolo persisted, sure that informed people armed with top-quality self-help information did not have to depend on lawyers. Over the years, more than three million customers have proven us right. Today, Nolo publishes over 100 self-help law books, audio tapes, videos and software packages—and is more committed than ever to making the law accessible.

About the Authors

ELY NEWMAN left his ancestral homeland in the Bronx for the golden shores of the San Francisco Bay over 20 years ago. A product of public schools and universities, he strives to write users' guides that even you can understand.

MARCIA STEWART, a Nolo author and editor, is an expert on landlord-tenant law, buying and selling houses, and other issues of interest to consumers. She is the co-author of Nolo's *Every Landlord's Legal Guide* and *Every Tenant's Legal Guide.* Marcia received a Master's degree in Public Policy from the University of California at Berkeley and has written and edited a wide variety of consumer publications for government agencies and private businesses.

RALPH WARNER is the co-founder and publisher of Nolo Press. He is the author of a number of self-help law titles, including *Everybody's Guide to Small Claims Court, The Partnership Book* (with Denis Clifford) and many landlord-tenant and real estate publications, including *Every Landlord's Legal Guide* (with Marcia Stewart and Janet Portman). Ralph is a lawyer who became fed up with the legal system. As a result, he has dedicated his professional life to making the legal system more accessible and affordable to all Americans.

JANET PORTMAN, an attorney and Nolo author and editor, received undergraduate and graduate degrees from Stanford and a law degree from the University of Santa Clara. She is an expert on landlord-tenant law and the co-author of *Every Landlord's Legal Guide* and *Every Tenant's Legal Guide.* As an attorney, she specialized in criminal defense, conducting trials and preparing and arguing appeals before the Court of Appeal and the California Supreme Court. Janet is the editor of several Nolo books, including *Legal Research: How to Find and Understand the Law.*

LEASEWRITER™

Users' Guide
by Ely Newman

Windows 　 Macintosh

Table of Contents

1 Welcome to *LeaseWriter*

2 Installing and Starting *LeaseWriter*

3 An Overview of *LeaseWriter*

7 Creating Additional Forms and Letters

8 Troubleshooting

Appendix: List of Forms in *LeaseWriter*

Index

CHAPTER

Welcome to *LeaseWriter*

Welcome to *LeaseWriter*, a comprehensive, easy-to-use program designed specifically for owners and managers of residential rental property.

With *LeaseWriter* you can handle every phase of the rental process from move-in to move-out. Using *LeaseWriter* makes it a snap to:
- create key documents every landlord needs
- get instant access to your state's landlord-tenant laws
- protect yourself and your rental property.

Landlords Who Should Not Use This Program

LeaseWriter is not designed for use by landlords who rent:
- property subsidized by the government (for example, Section 8 housing)
- mobile homes
- condominiums
- hotels
- commercial property.

LeaseWriter should be used by owners and managers of residential rental property only.

A. About This Manual

1. The Two Parts of the *LeaseWriter* Manual

This manual is divided into two main parts:

The first part is the Users' Guide, which explains how to use the *LeaseWriter* computer program. An electronic version of this users' guide is also incorporated into the program itself.

The second part of this manual is a version of the acclaimed book *Leases & Rental Agreements*, by Marcia Stewart and Attorneys Ralph Warner and Janet Portman (Nolo Press), designed especially for *LeaseWriter* users. This edition of *Leases & Rental Agreements* is a nuts-and-bolts guide to drafting a lease and other key documents in a tenancy. It provides legal and practical advice on screening tenants, returning deposits and more.

While you do not need to read the *Leases & Rental Agreements* book to use the *LeaseWriter* program, many landlords will find it useful to do so because *Leases & Rental Agreements*:

- shows how to prepare a lease or rental agreement on a clause-by-clause basis
- includes filled-in samples for all the forms in *LeaseWriter*, so you can easily see how a completed lease, rental application, security deposit itemization and other key documents should look
- provides a handy reference guide for you to quickly find legal and practical advice on choosing a tenant, ending a tenancy and other vital issues when you're away from your computer.

Note: The lease and other sample documents included in *Leases & Rental Agreements* are similar, but not identical, to the forms in *LeaseWriter*. Use these samples for illustrative purposes.

2. Typeface Conventions Used

This users' guide provides instructions on menus to select, buttons and icons to click, and keys to press. To make these instructions easier to follow, we use the following typeface conventions:

- **Buttons** and **icons** are in bold type.
- <u>Hypertext</u> is underlined, just as it appears on screen when you use the program.
- The first letters of names of Menus and Menu Commands are capitalized.
- KEYS that you are supposed to press are in SMALL CAPS.
- Key stroke combinations are conjoined by a "+"; for example "ALT+F4" means "hold down the ALT key while simultaneously pressing the F4 key."

3. A Special Note to Macintosh Users

This users' guide is for both Windows and Macintosh users. We have designed *LeaseWriter* so that it is virtually identical on both platforms. For this reason, the manual contains illustrations ("screen shots") from the Windows versions that apply to the Mac version as well.

Whenever the Windows and Macintosh versions differ significantly, we include specific instructions for Mac users.

Users' Guide

B. System Requirements

1. For Windows

To run *LeaseWriter* on a Windows system, you need:
- Operating System: Windows 95 or higher
- Processor/MHz: 486/33 or faster
- RAM: 8 MB (16 MB recommended)
- Hard Disk Space: 10 MB (20 to install)
- Monitor: 640 x 480
- CD-ROM Drive (for installation)
- a printer
- a mouse.

2. For Macintosh

To run *LeaseWriter* on a Macintosh, you need:
- Operating System: System 7.1 or higher
- Processor/MHz: Mac 68030 (68040 or higher recommended)
  RAM: 8 MB (16 MB recommended)
- Hard Disk Space: 10 MB (20 to install)
- Monitor: 640 x 480
- CD-ROM Drive (for installation)
- a printer
- a mouse.

If You Need to Install From Floppy Disks

If you are a registered user and would prefer to install the program from 3-1/2" floppy disks, contact Nolo Press Customer Service:
- Phone 800-992-6656
- E-mail cs@nolo.com
- Fax 510-548-5902.

There will be a small fee to cover shipping and handling.

C. *LeaseWriter* Package Contents

Your *LeaseWriter* package should contain:
- one dual-platform CD
- this *LeaseWriter* manual, and
- a registration card.

D. Register Your Copy

Registered owners of Nolo products receive a variety of free services and benefits.

But to provide these services, we need to know who you are. Please take the time now to complete and return the registration card included in the box, or the "electronic" form that's installed with the program. If you purchased *LeaseWriter* directly from Nolo Press (by phone or from our Website), you are already registered and don't need to send it in.

We also would appreciate any comments you have on *LeaseWriter*. We read every comment on every registration card.

E. Customer Service

Phone 510-549-1976 or 1-800-992-6656
Hours 9:00 A.M. to 5:00 P.M. Pacific Time, Monday through Friday
E-mail cs@nolo.com

Nolo Customer Service representatives can answer questions on product availability, prices, software upgrades, product features, customer registration, policies, procedures and other nontechnical topics.

Change of Address

If you move, please send a letter with both your old and new addresses and, if possible, the mailing code on your *Nolo News* mailing label to:

Customer Service
Nolo Press
950 Parker Street
Berkeley, CA 94710-9867
ATTN: CHANGE OF ADDRESS

Defective or Damaged Products

If you are a registered user and your disk is damaged or defective, we'll replace it free of charge. Send the defective disk and a brief explanation to:

Customer Service
Nolo Press
950 Parker Street
Berkeley, CA 94710-9867
ATTN: REPLACEMENT DISK

F. Technical Support

Nolo Press offers technical support for *LeaseWriter* to registered users only.

Phone   510-549-4660
Hours   9:00 A.M. to 5:00 P.M. Pacific Time, Monday through Friday
E-mail   NoloTec@nolo.com

If you have technical questions or problems operating this program, read Chapter 8, *Troubleshooting*, before contacting the Nolo Technical Support Department. ∎

CHAPTER

2

Installing and Starting *LeaseWriter*

I n this chapter, you'll learn how to install, start and exit the program.

A. Installing *LeaseWriter*

1. Windows

You will need approximately 20 MB of free space on your hard disk to install *LeaseWriter* for Windows and its accompanying help files. Once installed, the program will take up about 10 MB on your hard drive.

1. Start your computer.
2. Insert the *LeaseWriter* disk into your CD-ROM drive.
3. Follow the instructions that appear on the "Welcome to *LeaseWriter*" screen.

2. Macintosh

You will need approximately 20 MB of free space on your hard disk to install *LeaseWriter* for Macintosh and its accompanying help files. Once installed, the program will take up about 10 MB on your hard drive.

1. Start up your Macintosh.
2. Insert the *LeaseWriter* disk into your CD-ROM drive.
3. Double-click the **LeaseWriter Installer** icon.
4. Follow the instructions that appear on the screen.

3. Read the Read Me File

The *LeaseWriter* program folder that's created upon installation contains a Read Me file. Read this file to see important information that didn't make it into this manual. You should read this file before you start up *LeaseWriter*.

B. Starting *LeaseWriter*

Once you've installed *LeaseWriter* on your hard disk, you're ready to start the program.

1. Windows

1. Click the **Start** button in the task bar.
2. Point to Programs to open the Programs folder.
3. Point to **LeaseWriter 1.0** to open the *LeaseWriter* application folder.
4. Click the **LeaseWriter 1.0** application icon.

2. Macintosh

1. Open the folder that contains the *LeaseWriter* application by double-clicking it.
2. Double-click the **LeaseWriter 1.0** application icon.

Be Patient Waiting for the Program to Load

The *LeaseWriter* program is actually 24 related databases. When you start the program, all 24 databases are loaded. This can take several seconds—even on the fastest of computers. So be patient, please.

3. After You Start Up *LeaseWriter*

The program will start and you should see the opening screen shown below. If the opening screen doesn't appear, consult Chapter 8 of the Users' Manual.

At the opening screen, click **Continue.**

If you're using *LeaseWriter* for the first time, you'll then view an introduction to the program (see Section C, below).

If you've used *LeaseWriter* and viewed the introduction, you'll go to *LeaseWriter*'s Main Menu screen. From there you can select whether to:

- record **Rental Property Information** (see Chapter 5)
- **Create or Change a Lease** (see Chapter 6)
- create other **Forms & Letters** (see Chapter 7).

C. Using the Program for the First Time

The Introduction to *LeaseWriter* provides an overview of what's in the program and how to use it. By default, first-time users must go through this section once.

At the end of the Introduction, you're asked to enter your name. This "landlord's name" is added to your database and will show up as the "current landlord" when you begin creating your documents. (You can add other landlord names at any time.) After typing in your name, click the **Next** button.

After completing the Introduction, you'll go to *LeaseWriter*'s Main Menu screen. From there you can choose whether to:

- record **Rental Property Information** (see Chapter 5)
- **Create or Change a Lease** (see Chapter 6)
- create other **Forms & Letters** (see Chapter 7).

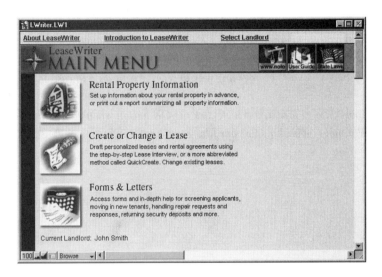

Be sure to read Chapter 3 of this Users' manual *before* you start entering information into *LeaseWriter*.

 Another way to read the Introduction to *LeaseWriter*. *To view the Introduction at any time:*

1. *Go to the Main Menu screen.*
2. *Click <u>Introduction to LeaseWriter</u> at the top of the screen.*

D. Exiting the Program

1. Windows

To exit *LeaseWriter* for Windows:
- choose Exit from the File menu, or
- press ALT+F4.

2. Macintosh

To quit *LeaseWriter* for Macintosh:
- choose Quit from the File menu, or
- press COMMAND + Q.

Back up your data when you exit. *Each time you exit, you'll see a dialog box asking if you want to back up your data. Although this process takes 10-15 seconds, we strongly recommend that you back up your data. If you do not create backup files, you will not have any way to recover your data in case of an unexpected crash.*

To export data to the backup files, click the **OK** *button when you see the Backup dialog box. For more on backing up your files, see Chapter 8, Section E.* ■

CHAPTER

3

An Overview of *LeaseWriter*

We've done our best to make *LeaseWriter* intuitive and easy-to-use. Nonetheless, before using the program, we suggest you read this chapter, which provides an overview of what's in *LeaseWriter* and answers to questions you're likely to have as you use *LeaseWriter*.

A. What's in *LeaseWriter*

The *LeaseWriter* program is divided into three main sections:

- **Rental Property Information** In this section, you record important information about your rental properties, such as addresses and rents. This information is automatically inserted when you create leases and other documents with *LeaseWriter*. For details on how to use this section of the program, and why you should set up property in advance, see Chapter 5.
- **Create or Change a Lease** In this section, you can create custom fixed-term leases and month-to-month rental agreements. You can also print out a lead hazard disclosure form. For details on how to use this section of the program, see Chapter 6.
- **Forms & Letters** In this section, you can create a dozen other key documents every landlord and property manager needs, including rental applications, repair request forms, forms for returning security deposits, and more. For details on how to use this section of the program, see Chapter 7.

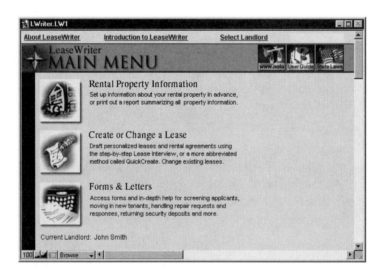

For the most part, *LeaseWriter* uses a simple interview format. For each document, you'll go through a series of custom screens, with specific instructions on how to enter the information *LeaseWriter* needs to create your documents. You can access any of these sections by using the Main Menu screen, which is accessible from all *LeaseWriter* program screens. The Appendix to this Users' Guide lists all the forms you can create using *LeaseWriter*.

In addition to these three sections, *LeaseWriter* includes an extensive Help system, which provides:

- legal help on how and when to use leases and other documents
- summaries of landlord-tenant law in all 50 states (50-State Law Browser)
- a version of this Users' Guide for help on how to use the program
- access to state statutes and codes on the Internet.

For details on how to get help from *LeaseWriter*, see Chapter 4.

B. Frequently Asked Questions About *LeaseWriter*

To familiarize you with how *LeaseWriter* works, and to anticipate your questions as you use the program, this section provides answers to FAQs *LeaseWriter* users are likely to have. Some of these may not make much sense until you've actually started using the program. Nonetheless, we suggest you give them a quick read now, and return to this section as needed to find answers to your questions. Of course, more detailed information about using *LeaseWriter* is included in the subsequent chapters—Chapter 6, for example, provides answers to frequently asked questions about entering information to create *LeaseWriter* leases.

1. What are all the files that are installed?

When you install the *LeaseWriter* program (see Chapter 2, Section A) you install an executable file and 24 related databases that comprise the program. The database files have the extension .LW1 (in Windows) or .FP3 (in Macintosh) at the end. *All* these files are opened automatically each time you start the program. In addition, seven backup files are installed (see Chapter 8, Section E).

2. Why are most of the menus disabled?

LeaseWriter was created using the FileMaker Pro development kit. The full FileMaker Pro application has features and capabilities beyond those included in this program. We've only included features that you need, and have disabled those that are unnecessary or problematic. All *LeaseWriter*'s functions and features are accessible using the icons, buttons and hypertext included in *LeaseWriter*'s program screens.

3. Why is the "Close" button in the title bar of program windows disabled?

In addition to the LeaseWriter window (the window that has "LeaseWriter" in its title bar), each related database (*.LW1 files in Windows; *.FP3 in Macintosh) runs in its own window. The main program window is LWriter; it has "LWriter.LW1" ("LWriter.FP3" in Macintosh) in its title bar.

The Close (x) button in the upper-right corner of its title bar is disabled on it and all *.LW1 (*.FP3 in Macintosh) program windows because all these files must stay open when you run *LeaseWriter*.

Disabled Close (X) button

4. What does the "Window" menu do?

The Window menu, which lists all the related databases (*.LW1 files in Windows; *.FP3 in Macintosh) in *LeaseWriter*, is of no use to users. DO NOT USE THE WINDOW MENU LOCATED AT THE TOP OF THE SCREEN.

5. Can I minimize the main program window?

Do not minimize the main program window (LWriter.LW1 or LWriter.FP3).

If you minimize the main program window, the *LeaseWriter* program window remains open and you'll see 24 minimized *LeaseWriter* database windows.

If you try to restore any of these windows, you'll see a message "Click anywhere to return to the program." Follow these instructions to restore the main program window.

6. How do I save my data?

Because it's entered directly into the *LeaseWriter* database, your information is saved automatically whenever you leave the screen in which you entered it—whether you go on to the next or the previous screen. So you don't need to use an additional "save" command to save your data. You should, however, back up your data when you exit (see Chapter 2, Section D).

7. Do I need to retype the same information each time I create a new document?

Not necessarily. When you enter information at a specific screen, *LeaseWriter* "knows" what other documents make use of the same information, and inserts such information automatically. You'll often find that when you create a document in the Forms & Letters section for the first time (see Chapter 7), some of the required information is already filled in.

8. Can I move from screen to screen using my keyboard?

No. To move from one *LeaseWriter* screen to another, you must use your mouse to click on the **Next** and **Back** buttons. You cannot move from screen to screen by pressing the ENTER or RETURN keys on your keyboard.

9. How can I make sure that my documents will comply with the laws of my state?

To make sure that your documents comply with the laws of your state, use *LeaseWriter*'s 50-State Law Browser. It contains summaries of relevant landlord-tenant law for all 50 states. Read these summaries to make sure that the provisions of your *LeaseWriter* documents comply with your state's legal requirements. For details on using *LeaseWriter*'s 50-State Law Browser, see Chapter 4, Section C.

In addition, *LeaseWriter* provides state-specific information, when appropriate, throughout the Lease Interview section of the program. Such information is highlighted in red. For details on using the Lease Interview, see Chapter 6, Section B.

> **EXAMPLE:** *If you're creating a lease for rental property in California, when you come to the screen where you specify the amount of the security deposit, you'll see California's deposit limits (usually two months' rent, with exceptions explained).*

Be aware that laws change, and in time some of the information in *LeaseWriter* may become out-of-date. If in doubt, consult a local attorney specializing in landlord-tenant law.

10. Can I create leases under different names?

Yes. You can enter as many "landlord" names as necessary. To do this: (1) go to the Main Menu; (2) click <u>Select Landlord</u>; (3) follow the instructions on adding and selecting landlords.

11. Can I change the font and other formatting on my documents?

No. Font type and size, margins and all other formatting for *LeaseWriter* documents cannot be changed. But don't worry—*LeaseWriter's* default formatting for these simple documents is more than adequate.

12. Can I open my documents in a word processor?

No. There is no way to export documents or open them in other applications. Among other things, this prevents you from creating legal problems by changing the language of your documents.

13. How are the documents produced by *LeaseWriter* related to the samples in the *Lease & Rental Agreements* book?

The same attorneys and authors who wrote the book *Lease & Rental Agreements* (provided free as a bonus if you bought a boxed version of *LeaseWriter*) worked to develop the program. The language in the forms is not identical, however; the book's documents are provided as samples for illustrative purposes. ◼

CHAPTER

Getting Help From *LeaseWriter*

*L*ease*Writer*'s Help system offers several different kinds of assistance:

- context-sensitive Legal Help topics, listed on the right side of most program screens, offer the legal and practical guidance for the particular screen you are viewing and document you are creating
- an electronic version of the User Guide, accessible from every program screen, gives you point-and-click access to the text of this manual
- state-by-state summaries of relevant codes and statutes
- easy access to your state's rental codes and statutes on the Internet.

Help Is Always Open

LeaseWriter's Help system works differently than the Help systems of most programs you're familiar with. It is not a separate file running in a separate application, that you can open and close separately.

Instead, *LeaseWriter*'s Help system is three of the 24 related databases that make up the *LeaseWriter* program. And like all *LeaseWriter*'s databases, the Help system is opened when you launch the program and remains open until you exit.

A. Viewing Legal Help Topics for Creating Your Documents

It's easy to view *LeaseWriter*'s Legal Help where and when you need it.

On the right side of most program screens, including the Lease Interview in the Create and Change a Lease section (see Chapter 6, Section B), there's a list of topics that offer the legal and practical guidance for the current screen. The listed topics are underlined hypertext.

To view a listed Help Topic, just click on it.

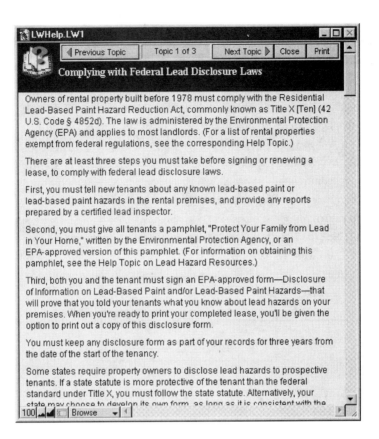

- To move up or down the current topic, use the scroll bar or the PAGEUP and PAGEDOWN keys.
- To maximize or minimize the Help window, use the system buttons in the Help window's title bar.
- To view the previous related topic, click the **Previous Topic** button in the Help window's tool bar.
- To view the next related topic, click the **Next Topic** button in the Help window's tool bar.
- To print the current topic, click the **Print** button in the Help window's tool bar.
- To bring the main program window back on top, click the **Close** button in the Help window's tool bar.

Using the Green ? Icon to View Legal Help

On certain screens where you enter information that is later used to create documents, there's another way to access to context-sensitive Legal Help topics. On the right of such screen is a green **?** icon. When you click the **?** icon, you'll see a Help Topic listing all Topics related to the information you are entering. The listed topics are underlined hypertext.

To view a listed Help Topic, just click on it.

To return to the list of related Help Topics:

1. Click the Help window's **Close** button to bring the main Program window back on top.

2. Click on the same **?** icon you clicked on to display the related Help Topics list.

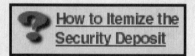

B. Viewing *LeaseWriter's* User Guide

LeaseWriter has an electronic version of this user's guide, accessible from every program screen, that gives you point-and-click access help on how to use the program.

To view the user's guide:

1. Click on the **User Guide** icon at the top of every main program screen. This opens a table of contents. All listed chapters are underlined hypertext.

2. Click on an underlined chapter to view a table of contents for that chapter. The listed topics are underlined hypertext.

3. To view a listed Users' Guide Topic, just click on it.

   • To move up or down the current topic, use the scroll bar or the PageUp and PageDown keys.

   • To maximize or minimize the User Guide window, use the system buttons in the User Guide window's title bar.

   • To view the previous related topic, click the **<** button in the User Guide window's tool bar.

- To view the next topic, click the **>** button in the Help window's tool bar.
- To print the current topic, click the **Print** button in the Help window's tool bar.
- To bring the main program window back on top, click the **Close** button in the User Guide window's tool bar.
- To return to the table of contents for the current chapter, click the **Chapter Contents** button in the User Guide window's tool bar.
- To return to the User Guide's Table of Contents, click the **Main Contents** button in the User Guide window's tool bar.

C. Using the 50-State Law Browser

To better help you understand the laws that control the business of landlording in your state, we've included summaries for every state.

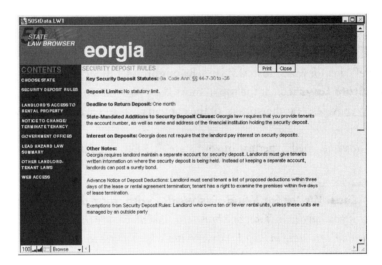

To see a summary of the rental laws for your state:

1. Click the **State Laws** icon at the top of most *LeaseWriter* main program windows. This opens a table of contents of *LeaseWriter*'s 50-State Law Browser. You'll see a list of legal categories, including Security Deposit Rules and Landlord's Access to Rental Property. All listed categories are underlined hypertext.
2. If your state's name appears at the top of the screen, go to Step 4.
   If you have not already selected your state, do so by first clicking **Choose State**, and then clicking on the underlined name of the state you're interested in.
3. You'll then return to the table of contents for your state. Your state's name should appear at the top of the screen which lists the same categories as in Step 1 on the left side of the window.

4. To view a summary, click on its legal category (for example, <u>Security Deposit Rules</u>).
   - To maximize or minimize the Browser window, use the system buttons in the Browser window's title bar.
   - To view a different summary for your state, click on its category on the left side of the window.
   - To view a different state's summaries, click <u>Choose State</u>.
   - To print the current summary, click the **Print** button in the Browser window's tool bar.
   - To bring the main program window back on top, click the **Close** button in the Browser window's tool bar.
   - To access your state's rental laws and statutes on the Internet, click <u>Web Access</u> (see Section D, below).

D. Getting Help From the Internet

If you have Internet access, you can use *LeaseWriter* to access your state's rental laws and statutes on the Web. Unfortunately, not all states have such Websites at this time.

1. If your default Web browser is not already running, start it. (Mac users can skip this step; *LeaseWriter* for Macintosh will launch your browser in Step 4, below.)
2. Click the **State Laws** icon at the top of most *LeaseWriter* main program windows.
3. Click on <u>Web Access</u> (at the bottom of the contents list) to see a listing of Websites for each state.
4. Click on the underlined hypertext of your state's URL to open that link in your Web browser.

> ⚠️ ***LeaseWriter* for Windows works with your default browser.**
> *If you have more than one browser installed, be sure that your default browser is the one that's running in Step 1. LeaseWriter's Web access feature will not work with a browser that is not your default browser.*

Launching Your Browser Running Macintosh System 7

Mac System 7 users cannot just click on a URL in this part of the 50 State Law Browser to launch their web browser and go to that location. Here's how to use *LeaseWriter's* Web Access feature if you're running Macintosh System 7:

1. Launch your web browser as you normally would.
2. Return to the Web Access section of *LeaseWriter's* 50 State Law Browser and click the URL of the site you want to go to. This copies the URL to your clipboard.
3. Return to your browser, paste the URL into your browser's Address field, and press the RETURN key. ∎

CHAPTER

Rental Property Information

Good record keeping is essential to any business—including landlording. Use the Rental Property Information section of *LeaseWriter* to document and track vital information about your rental properties and your tenants. As you'll see, "setting up" property in this section of the program in advance makes it even easier to create a lease and other documents in other sections of the program.

To go to the Property Information section of *LeaseWriter:*

1. Click the **Main Menu** button at the top of the *LeaseWriter* window.
2. Click the **Rental Property Information** icon on the left of the Main Menu screen.

You'll come to the Property Information Menu screen shown below.

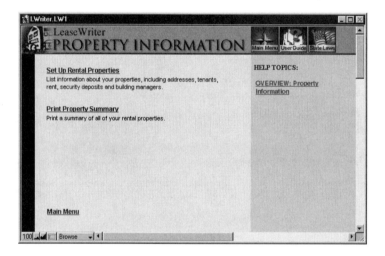

Use this screen to access the sections where you:

- **Set Up Rental Properties** by recording key information about your properties, rents, tenants, and building managers, and
- **Print a Property Summary** of this information.

These two sections are discussed in detail below.

A. Why You Should Set Up Property in Advance

While you can create *LeaseWriter* leases (Chapter 6) and other documents (Chapter 7) without setting up property in advance, we recommend you do so. Why? Because it makes creating leases and other documents later quicker and simpler.

Information entered when you set up property is stored in *LeaseWriter*'s database. Relevant data about these properties, like addresses and rents, are automatically inserted when you create *LeaseWriter* documents using other section of the program. So you won't need to retype or trust your memory of important details.

In addition, you'll be able to print out summaries of your rental property, as discussed in Section C, below.

B. Setting Up Rental Property

To go to the section of *LeaseWriter* where you enter information about your properties:
1. Click the **Main Menu** button at the top of the *LeaseWriter* window.
2. Click the **Rental Property Information** icon on the left of the Main Menu screen.
3. Click Set Up Properties.

What happens next depends on whether or not you have previously set up or entered property into the *LeaseWriter* database.

1. Adding Your First Property to *LeaseWriter*'s Database

If you're adding your first property to *LeaseWriter*'s database, you'll see the Add Properties screen, where you'll be prompted to type information into a blank list. The sequence varies for single- and multi-unit properties.

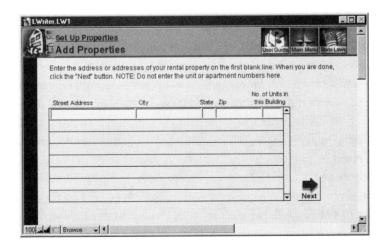

a. Adding a Single-Unit Building

1. At the Add Property screen, follow the instructions and type in all the required information. As soon as you go to the next data entry field, a new blank line is created immediately below the current one. Ignore the new blank line—you will type in it when you want to add your next property (here, we're suggesting you add one property at a time). Be sure to enter the number of rental units at this property. When done, click **Next**.

2. At the Select a Property screen, click on the listed property (the one you just entered) and click **Next**.

3. At the Information About the Property screen, follow the instructions and enter the information you're asked for. Some information that you entered on the previous screen appears on this one as well. Some of the fields (State, Number of Units) have drop-down lists you can select your answers from. When done, click **Next**.

4. At the More Information About the Rental Unit screen, follow the instructions and enter the information you're asked for. The Type of Unit field has a drop-down list you can select your answer from. When done, click **Next**.

5. You'll return to the Select a Property screen (Step 2), only now the one listed property is checked, indicating that you have completed setting it up.
   At this point you can:

   • continue setting up additional properties by clicking <u>Add Properties</u> or,
   • end this process and leave this section of the program by clicking <u>Done Adding Properties</u>.

b. Adding a Multi-Unit Property

1. At the Add Property screen, follow the instructions and type in all the required information. As soon as you go to the next data entry field, a new blank line is created immediately below the current one. Ignore the new blank line—you will type in it when you want to add your next property. Be sure to enter the number of rental units at this address. When done, click **Next**.

2. At the Select a Property screen, click on the listed property (the one you just entered) and click **Next**.

3. At the Information About the Property screen, follow the instructions and enter the information you're asked for. Some information that you entered on the previous screen appears on this one as well. Some of the fields (State, Number of Units) have drop-down lists you can select answers from. When done, click **Next**.

4. At the Units at [Your Address] screen, follow the instructions and enter the information you're asked for each unit. As soon as you go to the first data entry field, a new blank line is created immediately below the current one. Ignore the new blank line for now— you will type in it when you want to enter information about the next unit at that address. Be sure to click Add Tenants Names and enter that information. When you're finished entering all units, click **Next**.

5. You'll return to the Select a Property screen (Step 2), only now the one listed property is checked, indicating that you have completed setting it up.

At this point you can:
- continue setting up additional properties by clicking Add Properties or,
- end this process and leave this section of the program by clicking Done Adding Properties.

2. Adding More Properties

The sequence for adding properties is different for single-unit and multi-unit buildings.

To add a single-unit property at the Select a Property screen:
1. Click Add Properties.
2. Follow the instructions in Section 1a, above.

To add a multi-unit property at the Select a Property screen:
1. Click Add Properties.
2. Follow the instructions in Section 1b, above.

3. Deleting and Modifying Properties That Were Set Up Previously

To delete a property that was set up previously:

1. Click the **Main Menu** button at the top of the *LeaseWriter* window.
2. Click the **Rental Property Information** icon on the left of the Main Menu screen.
3. Click Set Up Properties to go to the Select a Property screen.
4. At the Select a Property screen, select the property you want to delete by clicking on it, then click Delete Property.
5. You'll see a dialog box asking whether you want to delete this property and its associated records. Click **Delete**.

You'll return to the Select a Property screen (Step 4); the property you deleted will no longer be listed.

To add or change information about a property that was set up previously:

1. Click the **Main Menu** button at the top of the *LeaseWriter* window.
2. Click the **Rental Property Information** icon on the left of the Main Menu screen.
3. Click <u>Set Up Properties</u> to go to the Select a Property screen.
4. At the Select a Property screen, select the property you want to change information about by clicking on it, then click **Next**.
5. At the Information About the Property and More Information About the Rental Unit screens, revise the information you've already entered into the appropriate fields. When done, click **Next**.

You'll return to the Select a Property screen (Step 4).

C. Printing Out Property Summaries

You can print out summaries of the information you've entered into the Rental Property Information section of *LeaseWriter* or in the Create or Change a Lease section (Chapter 6).

1. What's Included in the Summary

In addition to the total monthly rent for all units, the summary lists each unit's:

- address
- type (studio, one bedroom, etc.)
- amount of rent
- amount of security deposit
- term of lease
- start date of lease
- end date of lease (if applicable)
- names of tenants
- contact phone number for tenants
- building manager information (if appropriate).

Property Owned by John Smith
Total Monthly Rent from All Units: $1,000
Printed Thursday, August 27, 1998 at 3:21:05 PM

1234 First St. Berkeley. CA 98765
No. of Units: 1
Manager: Joe Average 1234 First St. Berkeley, CA 98765
    Day Phone: (123) 456-7890 Eve Phone: (456) 123-7890
    Fax: (321) 654-0987 Pager: (654) 321-7890
    Email: averagejoe@aol.com

              Type: Rent: Deposit: Lease Term: Start Date: End Date:
              2 BR $1,000 $950   8/27/98

Current Tenants: John Doe, Jane Doe and John Jr.
No. to Contact: (123) 555-1111

If information is missing in the summary. *In order for all the information about a property to appear in this summary, you must have entered all this information when you set up the property, as described in Section A. To add the missing information, follow the instructions in Section A on setting up property.*

2. How to Print the Property Summary

To print a summary of the properties you've entered into *LeaseWriter*:

1. Click the **Main Menu** button at the top of the *LeaseWriter* window.
2. Click the **Rental Property Information** icon on the left of the Main Menu screen.
3. Click <u>Print Property Summary</u>.
4. The Summary document will then open in *LeaseWriter*'s Document Preview window. The first page of the summary is shown.
   - Use the scroll bar to view the entire page.
   - To view the next page, click on the bottom page of the **Notebook** icon in the upper left corner.
   - To return to a previous page, click on the top page of the **Notebook** icon in the upper left corner.
5. Click the **Continue** button in the middle of the left side of the screen.
6. At the dialog box that opens, click **Print**.

7. At the Print Setup (Windows) or Page Setup (Macintosh) dialog box, check to make sure the settings are correct, and make any necessary changes. When done, click **OK**.

8. At the Print dialog box that opens, click **Print**.

> ⚠ **The property summary is a print-only document.** *You cannot edit this document directly. If you want to correct or change any information in the Property Summary, you'll need to do so by going to the screen where you originally entered information, as described in Section B3, above.* ■

CHAPTER

6

Creating a Lease or Rental Agreement

Using *LeaseWriter* is the easiest way to create a custom lease or rental agreement. This chapter shows how to use the Create or Change a Lease section of the program to create leases and lead hazard disclosure documents.

To go to the Create or Change a Lease section of *LeaseWriter*:

1. Click the **Main Menu** button at the top of the *LeaseWriter* window.

2. Click the **Create or Change a Lease** icon on the left of the Main Menu screen.

You'll come to the Create a Lease screen shown below.

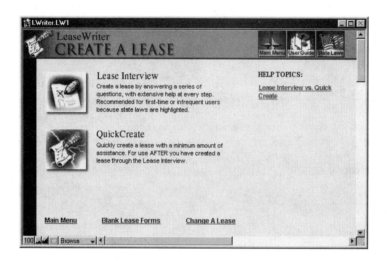

This screen offers a choice of two methods for creating a lease. Before making your selection, read Section A, *Two Methods for Creating a Lease*, below.

⚠ **Consult the 50-State Law Browser.** *While* LeaseWriter *cannot check that all your answers are in compliance with your state's laws, it provides a means for you to do so yourself—the 50-State Law Browser. We strongly suggest consulting its summaries of your state's laws as you create your documents. For details, see Chapter 4, Section C.*

If you're still in doubt as to the legality of any of the provisions in your lease documents, consult an attorney familiar with landlord-tenant law.

The Terms "Lease" and "Rental Agreement"

Throughout this chapter of the Users' Guide and the *LeaseWriter* program, the term "lease" refers to both leases and rental agreements. In reality, these two documents are different. *LeaseWriter* lets you create both fixed-term leases and month-to-month rental agreements. The difference between the two is explained in *Part 4, Term of Tenancy* of the Lease Interview (see Section B), when you're asked to choose which type of agreement you want to make.

A. Two Methods for Creating a Lease

LeaseWriter gives you a choice of two methods for creating a lease or rental agreement:
- the Lease Interview, a detailed, step-by-step approach, and
- QuickCreate, a faster, more direct approach.

Both the Lease Interview and QuickCreate produce comprehensive, legal rental agreements. There's no difference in the language of documents that result from either method.

If you're creating your first *LeaseWriter* lease, we strongly recommend that you select the Lease Interview method. In fact, until you have created several *LeaseWriter* leases and have fully familiarized yourself with the on-screen legal Help Topics, we suggest you only use QuickCreate to make minor changes to *LeaseWriter* leases you've already created. For details, see *Lease Interview vs. QuickCreate,* below.

Lease Interview vs. QuickCreate

What's the difference?

The screens you see during the Lease Interview contain detailed discussions of the legal issues involved in answering every question. In the Interview, you are prompted to enter information one screen at a time, and can see a summary of the details of the lease as you're drafting it. The Lease Interview also features easier access to all related Legal Help Topics. In addition, some Lease Interview screens provide state-specific information about the laws in your state that are relevant to the information you're being asked to enter.

In QuickCreate, you enter all the required information for your document on just a few screens. While all relevant Legal Help is accessible, getting it requires some additional effort (that is, more mouse clicks) on your part. In addition, QuickCreate screens do not provide state-specific information about relevant laws in your state, as some Lease Interview screens do (although while using the QuickCreate you can always look up your state's law in the 50-State Law Browser (see Chapter 4, Section C)).

Which method should you use?

Use Lease Interview if ...

- You're making your first *LeaseWriter* lease.
- You're making a new lease for property in a state in which you haven't already made several *LeaseWriter* leases.
- You're making revisions to a lease for property in a state in which you haven't already made several *LeaseWriter* leases.
- You're not a frequent *LeaseWriter* user.

Use QuickCreate if ...

- You're a frequent *LeaseWriter* user and are making minor revisions to a lease for property in a state in which you've previously created several *LeaseWriter* leases.
- You're a frequent *LeaseWriter* user and are creating a lease for property in a state in which you've previously created several *LeaseWriter* leases.

B. Using the Lease Interview to Create a Lease

To start the Lease Interview:

1. Click the **Main Menu** button at the top of the *LeaseWriter* window.
2. Click **Create or Change a Lease**.
3. Click **Lease Interview**.

You'll come to the Lease Interview Menu screen shown below.

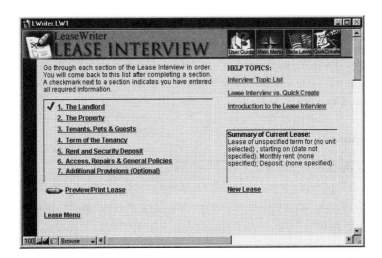

> 💡 **Read the Help.** *Before you begin the Lease Interview, read all the Help Topics listed on the right of the Lease Interview Menu screen. If it's your first time using the Lease Interview, we strongly suggest that you read all the Help Topics listed in each Interview screen before you go on to the next screen.*

In the remainder of this section, we discuss generally how to use this screen to complete the Interview and create your lease. For more detailed information on the individual components of the Lease Interview, read the Help Topics listed on the right of each screen.

1. Elements of the Lease Interview Menu Screen

From this screen, you have access to everything you'll need to create your lease.

a. The Seven Parts of the Lease Interview

On the left of the screen, the seven parts of the Interview are listed in order (Landlord, Property and so on). To start working on a listed part, just click on it. For details, see Section 3, *Completing the Interview Step-by-Step*, below.

In addition, this parts checklist provides access to the screen that you use to preview and print your completed document. For details, see Section E, *Displaying and Printing Your Lease Documents*, below.

b. Help Topics List

As on most *LeaseWriter* screens, there's a list of related Help Topics on the right. Just click on the underlined topic name to view that topic. For more information about the *LeaseWriter* Help system, see Chapter 4, G*etting Help From* LeaseWriter.

c. Lease Summary

On the right of the screen, just below the Help Topics list, is the Lease Summary. It summarizes the main components of the lease you're creating: address of the property, term of the lease, start date of lease, amount of rent and amount of security deposit. As you go through the Interview and enter information, it is added to this summary.

2. Navigating Through the Interview Screens

Within the interview there are two types of screens:
- "information" screens, which don't request any input from you, but provide important information on what you're about to do
- "data entry" screens, in which you must make a choice, answer a question or enter information that is incorporated into your document.

To move to the next screen, click **Next** or <u>Done</u> in the lower right. On some input screens, *LeaseWriter* will not let you go on to the next screen until you have entered the required information. When you move to the next screen after entering data on an input screen, that data is saved automatically.

To go back to the previous screen, click the **Back** button in the lower right of the screen.

From any screen in the Interview section you can return to the Lease Interview Menu screen (which includes the parts checklist and lease summary) by clicking the **Interview** icon at the top of the screen.

3. Completing the Interview Step-by-Step

To create a lease or rental agreement, you need to: (1) go through, *in order*, each of the seven parts of the Interview, and (2) enter the required information as directed on each interview screen.

To complete the seven interview parts of the Lease Interview:

1. Click <u>1. The Landlord</u> to confirm or change the information that's been entered into this section. (For an explanation of why this part is checked even though you haven't gone through this part, see Section D, below). When you're done, you'll return to the Lease Interview Menu screen.

2. Visit and complete each of the seven interview parts in order. Read each screen carefully and enter the required information.

You complete the Lease Interview by entering the information the program asks for. Each data entry screen contains specific instructions on the kind of information you need to enter and how to do so, and provides access to relevant Help Topics.

When you're done entering the required information on a particular screen, click **Next** or <u>Done</u> to go to the next step.

After you've entered all the information required to complete a part of the Interview, you'll return to the Lease Interview Menu screen. That part will be checked to indicate that the information required to complete your lease has been entered.

After you've completed Parts 1-6, you can print out your complete agreement (Part 7, which is optional, does not need to be completed). *See* Section E, *Displaying and Printing Your Lease Document*, below.

 Tips on entering information. *See Section D, below, for tips on entering information to create* LeaseWriter *leases.*

4. Printing Your Lease After You Complete the Interview

After you've answered all the Interview questions, you can print out your completed agreement. At the Lease Interview Menu screen, Parts 1-6 should be checked (as discussed above, Part 7, which is not required, is never checked).

Below the parts checklist, a "pencil" icon points to either <u>Preview/Print Lease</u> or <u>Ready to Print</u>.

- <u>Preview/Print Lease</u> means that some required information has been omitted. Click <u>Preview/Print Lease</u> to view a screen that tells you what information is missing, then click <u>Fix the problem</u>, and enter the required information. When done, click the

Lease Interview icon at the upper right to go back to the Lease Interview menu. If the pencil icon still points to Preview/Print Lease it means that there is an additional problem that needs fixing, as described above.

- Ready to Print means that all required information has been entered. Click Ready to Print to go to the Display & Print screen. At this screen, click Preview/Print Lease to open your document in the Print Preview Window. Go on to Section E, below, for details on displaying and printing your lease.

C. Creating a Lease With QuickCreate

As noted earlier, QuickCreate—the faster of the two ways to create or change a lease—is recommended for experienced *LeaseWriter* users only.

To get to *QuickCreate*:

1. Click the **Main Menu** button at the top of the *LeaseWriter* window.
2. Click **Create or Change a Lease**.
3. Click **QuickCreate**.

You'll come to the Select Property screen—the first part of the QuickCreate process.

There are four parts to the process of creating a lease using QuickCreate. Each part is discussed below. To go to any part, click the corresponding tab at the top of any QuickCreate screen.

1. Select Property

If you click on the **Select Property** tab, you'll see a list of all rental property you've entered into *LeaseWriter*. In this part you can:

- select the property the lease is for, if it is listed
- add properties to the list, or modify information about already-listed properties, and
- select the name of the landlord that will appear on the lease.

a. Selecting Property

If the property you want to select is listed, click on it.

- If you selected a single-unit dwelling, you're done selecting property and are ready to go to the Tenancy Information section, described below.
- If you selected a multi-unit dwelling, you'll be prompted to select the unit the lease is for. If you have not completely set up all the units for this property (see Chapter 5), you'll need to enter unit or apartment numbers for each unit before you can select a unit.
- If the property has not been entered yet, you'll need to click Edit or Add Property to add that property to the list so that you can make your selection (see below).

b. Adding or Modifying Property

If you need to add properties (because a property you want to create a lease for is not listed) or modify a listed property, here's how:

1. Click <u>Edit or Add Property</u>.
2. Enter all the additional properties you want to add.
3. When you're finished, click <u>Done Adding Property</u>.

If the property you've added is a multi-unit dwelling, you'll be prompted to enter the apartment or unit number for each and select the unit this lease is for (see above).

c. Selecting a Landlord

If the name of the landlord listed below the property list is not the name you want for this agreement, click <u>Select Landlord</u> and follow the directions on adding and modifying landlords' names.

⚠ **Selecting a landlord is done outside of QuickCreate.** *If you click <u>Select Landlord</u>, you'll be "kicked" out of the QuickCreate section of the program in order to make your selection. When you're done, you're returned to LeaseWriter's Main Menu. To go back to QuickCreate from there, first click the* **Create or Change Lease** *icon, then click the* **QuickCreate** *icon.*

d. When You've Completed This Section

When you've completed the Select Property section, you're automatically taken to the Tenancy Information Section, described below.

2. Tenancy Information and General Policies

These two sections are where you enter specific data about the terms of the lease you are creating. The table below shows what information is entered into each of these sections.

LEASE INFORMATION IN QUICKCREATE

Section	Subsections
Tenancy Information	rental term and start date
	tenant names
	rent amount
	security deposit
	furnishings
	included areas
	excluded areas
	pets
	lead paint hazard and other disclosures
General Policies	payment policies
	late rent fees
	attorney fees
	legal papers, people authorized to receive
	guests
	utilities
	notice to enter rental policy
	extended absence by tenants
	additional provisions
	tenant rules & regulations

a. How the Two Sections Differ

- **Tenancy Information** is where you enter and review lease information for the selected property that is specific to that tenancy—for example, the name of your tenant and the amount of rent.
- **General Policies** is where you enter and review general information for the selected property that is likely to be applied to other leases as well—for example, who's authorized to accept legal papers on your behalf or what utilities you will pay for.

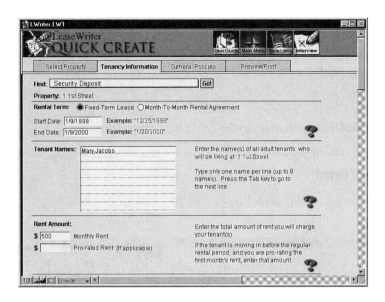

b. Entering Information in Your Lease

Use the scroll bar to go through each of the two sections and enter all the information needed to complete your lease. Be sure and consult the appropriate Help Topic(s) by clicking the green **?** icons on the right of the fields where you enter your information.

⚠ Consult the 50-State Law Browser. *While* LeaseWriter *cannot check that all of your answers are in compliance with your state's laws, it provides a means for you to do so yourself—the 50-State Law Browser. We strongly suggest consulting its summaries of your state's laws as you create your documents. For details, see Chapter 4, Section C.*
If you're still in doubt as to the legality of any of the provisions in your documents, consult an attorney familiar with landlord-tenant law .

💡 Tips on entering information. *See Section D, below, for tips for answers to frequently asked questions about entering information to create* LeaseWriter *leases.*

c. Searching for a Particular Field

If you want to search for a particular field, here's how:
1. Click on the **Find:** list (located at the top of the screen, just below the four QuickCreate tabs) to select the information you want to revise. For example, if you want to change the amount of rent, select "Rent Amount."
2. Click the **Go!** Button to move to the field where that information is located.

3. Preview/Print

After you click on the **Preview/Print** tab, you'll see the screen shown below.

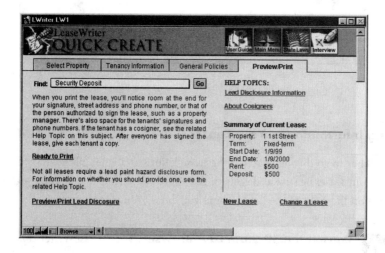

Use this screen to display and print out your lease and, if necessary, a lead disclosure form. You can also view a summary of the lease and related Help topics.

On the middle-left of the screen it will either say <u>Preview/Print Lease</u> or <u>Ready to Print</u>.

- <u>Preview/Print Lease</u> means that some required information has been omitted. Click <u>Preview/Print Lease</u> to view a screen that tells you what information is missing. Then, click <u>Fix the problem</u>, and enter the required information. When done, click on the **Preview/Print** tab. If it still says <u>Preview/Print Lease</u> it means that there is an additional problem that needs fixing, as described above.
- <u>Ready to Print</u> means that all required information has been entered. Click <u>Ready to Print</u> to open your document in the Print Preview Window. Go on to Section E, below, for details on displaying and printing your lease.

D. Tips on Entering Information to Create Leases

This section provides an overview on how to enter information into the data-entry screens in the Create or Change a Lease section of *LeaseWriter*.

1. Navigating Through *LeaseWriter* Using the Keyboard

At data-entry screens where there are two or more fields to enter information into, you can use your computer's keyboard to move from one field to another by pressing the TAB key until your cursor is in the field you want to type in.

After entering the requested information, do not try to use the ENTER or RETURN keys to move to the next screen. Pressing the ENTER or RETURN keys adds a hard carriage turn to the information you entered. To move to the next screen, use your mouse to click the **Next** button on the lower right of the *LeaseWriter* screen.

2. Saving Your Data

Because it's entered directly into the *LeaseWriter* database, your information is saved automatically whenever you leave the screen in which you entered it—whether you go on to the next or the previous screen. So there is no Save command for saving your data.

3. Doing the Lease Interview in Order

LeaseWriter needs to know your name and the property the lease is for before you can enter additional information. Therefore, you must complete Parts 1 (Landlord) and 2 (Property) before you can go to any of the other parts.

However, you may have entered the data needed for Part 1 when you entered your name the first time you started *LeaseWriter*. (See Chapter 2, Section C.)

Likewise, you may have already entered the data needed for Part 2 if you set up property in the Rental Property Information section of the program and entered your name the first time you started *LeaseWriter*. (See Chapter 5, Section B.)

After the information for Parts 1 and 2 is entered, you can randomly access any of the other Interview parts. We suggest, however, that you do the Interview in order.

4. Making Selections With Your Mouse

On data-entry screens where you can select a radio button or a checkbox, you must make your selection by clicking on the item with your mouse. You will not be able to use your keyboard to select a radio button or checkbox.

5. Leaving a Field or Screen Blank

Some of the information you're asked to enter is mandatory; some is optional. You needn't worry which is which because:
- *LeaseWriter* won't let you leave a screen where you need to enter mandatory information without doing so.
- *LeaseWriter* screens contain specific information on whether or not you can leave a question unanswered.

LeaseWriter won't let you print a lease that is missing mandatory information.

6. Why Is a Lease Interview Part Checked That Was Not Visited

LeaseWriter is a database program into which you enter a wide range of information about your rental properties. Data that you enter once may be used many times over, in other sections, without you having to enter it again. *LeaseWriter* "knows" when and where to incorporate previously entered information into your documents.

> **EXAMPLE 1:** *When you first started the program you were prompted to enter your name (at the Landlord's Name screen in the Introduction to LeaseWriter). So when you come to the Lease Interview parts checklist for the first time, 1. Landlord is checked.*

> **EXAMPLE 2:** *If you've created a lease for a unit in a multi-unit building and then begin creating a new lease for another unit in the same building, several parts are checked. LeaseWriter has already incorporated previously entered data about your name, the provisions that are dictated by the rental laws of your state, and your own policies for that building.*

Nonetheless, before printing out your lease you should visit each of the seven parts—whether checked or not—in order to:
- confirm that any information that has already been entered is correct, and
- add any information that has not been entered but is needed.

7. How Information Is Incorporated Into the Final Document

If you're used to creating a lease one clause at a time, *LeaseWriter*'s approach may seem odd at first. The *LeaseWriter* lease is not created by filling in the blanks of a document template in a word processor. Instead, you answer a series of questions needed to create a complete, comprehensive and legal agreement. When all your answers are in, your data are "assembled" into a complete, multiple-clause lease. You can preview the lease before you print it, as described in Section E, below.

To help you understand how your answers are used in the resulting document, read the Help Topic <u>Where This Information Is Used in the Lease</u> whenever it is available during the Lease Interview.

8. Punctuation in Data-Entry Fields

When *LeaseWriter* assembles your answers to create your lease, it adds the necessary punctuation. For example, if you put a period (.) after the last word in your answer, you may find that (because that word is the last word in a sentence in your lease) there are two periods at the end of the sentence.

Follow the on-screen examples on how to punctuate your answers.

9. Adding Provisions to the Standard *LeaseWriter* Lease

Both the Lease Interview (in Part 7) and QuickCreate (at the bottom of the General Policies screen) allow you to add your own custom provisions. Be sure and use the 50-State Law Browser to ensure that any additional provisions included in your lease comply with the laws of your state—*LeaseWriter* cannot verify whether any custom provisions are legal. If you're in doubt, have an attorney who specializes in landlord-tenant law look over your additional provisions.

10. Creating Different Leases Under Different Names

Some property owners do business under more than one name. You can make sure that each lease incorporates the correct name by entering all the names into the *LeaseWriter* database when you use the program for the first time.

You can add more names at any time. Go to the Main Menu screen and click <u>Select Landlord</u>. After entering a new landlord's name, it will be available whenever you need to create a lease—whether you use the Lease Interview or QuickCreate method.

11. Deleting Duplicate Properties

If you've accidentally entered the same property more than once, you should delete one of the properties. Don't try to do this in the Create a Lease section of the program. Instead, use the Main Menu to go to the Property Information section of *LeaseWriter* and follow the instructions on deleting property.

E. Displaying and Printing Your Lease Document

When you've finished entering your information, you can display the completed lease or agreement and print it out. This process is the same whether you've created your lease by using Lease Interview or QuickCreate section.

To display and print in the Lease Interview section:

1. Click the **Lease Interview** icon to return to the to the Lease Interview Menu screen.

2. At the Lease Interview Menu screen, click Ready to Print (next to the "pencil" icon).

To display and print in QuickCreate:

1. Click the **Preview/Print** tab at the top of the screen.

2. Click Ready to Print.

> **If it doesn't say ready to print.** *Ready to Print means that all required information has been entered. If it instead says Preview/Print Lease, you need to click there and follow the instructions on how to fix the problem and add the required information.*

Your lease will be assembled and displayed in a Document Preview Window.

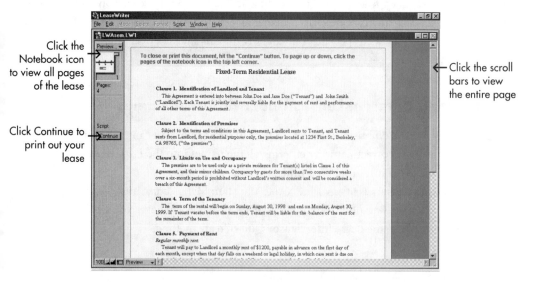

1. Displaying Your Lease

When you click <u>Ready to Print</u>, your lease opens in the Document Preview window. *LeaseWriter*'s document display is WYSIWYG—what you see is what you get. You cannot change the font type, font size, or do any kind of reformatting to change how your document will look when it is printed.

   While your document is displayed, you can view each page but cannot do any editing.

- To move around each page of the displayed document, use the scroll bar.
- To move to the next page, click the bottom page of the **Notebook** icon in the upper left of the Document Preview window.
- To go back to a previous page, click the top page of the **Notebook** icon in the upper left of the Document Preview window.
- If you're satisfied with your document and want to print it out, (1) click the **Continue** button on the left of the Document Preview window, then (2) click **Print**. For details see *Printing Your Lease*, below.
- If you want to revise your document by changing an Interview answer, (1) click the **Continue** button on the left of the Document Preview window, (2) click **Close** to return to the Printing/Displaying the Lease screen, and (3) click **Revise Current Lease.** For details see Section F, *Changing a Lease*, below.

2. Printing Your Lease

While your document is displayed, you can print it out. Note that you cannot change the font type, font size, or do any kind of reformatting to change how your document will look when it is printed.

   To print out a completed lease:

1. Display it in the Document Preview Window, as described in Section 1, above.
2. Click the **Continue** button on the left side of the document display window.
3. Click **OK** when you're asked if you want to print the lease.
4. At the Print Setup (Windows) or Page Setup (Macintosh) dialog box, check to make sure the settings are correct, and make any necessary changes. When done, click **OK**.
5. At the Print dialog box that opens, click **Print**.

F. Changing a Lease

You may find you need to make significant changes—such as raising the rent, adding a new tenant, or allowing a tenant to keep a pet—to your *LeaseWriter* lease or rental agreement.

> ⚠️ **Before you change a lease.** *Should you revise the lease? Add an addendum? Replace the old lease with a new one? Before you decide, read the Help Topic <u>Changing a Lease or Rental Agreement</u>.*
>
> **After you make a change.** *We suggest that you have a lawyer experienced in landlord-tenant law review any major changes to a lease, especially in the Additional Provisions clause.*

To go to the section of *LeaseWriter* where you can change your document:

1. Click the **Main Menu** button at the top of the *LeaseWriter* window.
2. Click **Create or Change a Lease**.
3. Click **Change a Lease**.

The next steps involved in making significant changes to a completed document are:

- selecting the property covered by the lease you want to change
- selecting the method—Lease Interview or QuickCreate
- changing the document information you entered previously.

These steps are discussed below.

1. Selecting Property

After clicking **Change a Lease,** as described above, you'll come to the Select Property screen, listing all properties and units you've entered so far into the *LeaseWriter* database.

To select a rental property:

1. Click on a listed property.
2. Click **Next**.

This will take you to the screen where you select which method you'll use to make the revisions.

2. Selecting the Method—Lease Interview or QuickCreate

After selecting the property, you'll come to the Select Method screen, offering you a choice of the Lease Interview or QuickCreate methods. If you're not sure which method to choose, and you haven't yet used QuickCreate, choose Lease Interview. To make your selection, click the corresponding button.

- If you select **Lease Interview**, go on to *Using the Lease Interview to Change Document Information*, below.
- If you select **QuickCreate**, go on to *Using QuickCreate to Change Document Information*, below.

3. Using the Lease Interview to Change Document Information

If you selected Lease Interview, you'll see the familiar Lease Interview menu. Parts 1-6 are checked and the pencil icon points to <u>Ready to Print</u>.

   To change information in the current lease:

1. Select the part of the Interview where you entered the information you want to revise. (For example, if you want to change the amount of rent, click <u>5. Rent and Security Deposit</u>.) For help locating the correct part, read the Help Topic <u>Interview Topic List</u>.
2. Click on the **Next** button until you reach the specific screen that contains the information you want to change.
3. Make the change(s) you want.
4. Review the other screens in that part until you return to the Lease Interview Menu screen.
   Repeat these steps to make additional changes. When you're done revising, you can print out and display the revised document (see Section E).

> **EXAMPLE:** *After creating a Lease Interview agreement for Apt. C at 1785 Townsend Ave., Lester Hawkins wants to change the move-in date from the first of May to the tenth. To do this Lester goes to the Create a Lease screen, then clicks <u>Change a Lease</u>. All four units are listed at the Select Property screen because, when he created the agreement, he entered the number of units at this property. He selects 1785 Townsend Ave., Apt C, then clicks* **Next.** *Since he's only created a LeaseWriter lease once before, he selects* **Lease Interview.** *To change the move-in-date, Lester: (1) goes to the Lease Interview section; (2) clicks <u>4. Term of Tenancy</u>; (3) at the Rental Agreement or Lease Start Date screen, changes "5/1/99" to "5/10/99."*
>
> *Having completed his revisions, he clicks the* **Interview** *icon in the upper right to return to Lease Interview Menu screen. From there he clicks <u>Ready to Print</u> and prints out the revised document.*

4. Using QuickCreate to Change Document Information

If you selected QuickCreate, you'll go to the Tenancy Information section of the QuickCreate screen.

   To change information in the current lease:

1. Click on the **Find:** drop-down list (located below the tabs) to select the information you want to revise (for example, if you want to change the amount of rent, select "Rent Amount").
2. Click the **Go!** button to move to the field where that information is located.
3. Make the change you want.

Repeat these steps to make additional changes. When you're done revising, you can print out and display the revised document.

> **EXAMPLE:** *After creating a QuickCreate agreement for Apt. C at 1785 Townsend Ave., Lester Hawkins wants to change the move-in date from the first of May to the tenth. To do this Lester goes to the Create a Lease screen, then clicks <u>Change a Lease</u>. All four units are listed at the Select Property screen because he has created leases for them all. He selects "1785 Townsend Ave., Apt. C," then clicks **Next**. Since he is an experienced user who has created* LeaseWriter *leases for other units in this building, he selects **QuickCreate**. At the Tenancy Information section, Lester: (1) clicks on the **Find:** drop-down list and selects "Tenancy Start Date;" (2) clicks the **Go!** button to move to the Start Date field; (3) changes "5/1/99" to "5/10/99."*
>
> *Having finished making his change, he clicks the **Preview/Print** tab, and then prints out the revised document.*

G. Creating Additional Leases

If you rent several units, you will undoubtedly need to create many *LeaseWriter* leases. Even if you own just one rental unit, over time one tenant will depart to be replaced by another, requiring a new agreement.

To go to the section of *LeaseWriter* where you can create a new lease:

1. Click the **Main Menu** button at the top of the *LeaseWriter* window.
2. Click **Create or Change a Lease**.

The next step involved in creating a new lease is selecting the method—Lease Interview or QuickCreate.

1. Selecting the Method—Lease Interview or QuickCreate

As recommended in the beginning of this chapter, use the Lease Interview until you have created several *LeaseWriter* leases and have fully familiarized yourself with the on-screen legal help topics. We suggest you use QuickCreate to create a new lease only if:

- you're an experienced *LeaseWriter* user
- you've already created a *LeaseWriter* lease for that property or for another unit in the same building, and
- the terms and conditions for the new lease will be similar to those of the previous *LeaseWriter* lease for this property or another unit in the same building.

To make your selection, click either the **Lease Interview** or the **QuickCreate** icon at the Create or Change a Lease screen.

- If you select **Lease Interview**, go on to *Using the Lease Interview to Create Additional Leases,* below.
- If you select **QuickCreate** go on to *Using QuickCreate to Create Additional Leases,* below.

2. Using the Lease Interview to Create Additional Leases

If you selected Lease Interview, you'll see the familiar Lease Interview menu.

To start creating a new lease

1. Click <u>New Lease</u> below the Lease Summary on the right side of the screen.
2. Click **OK** when asked if you want to create a new lease.

You'll return to the Lease Interview screen. Notice that all parts are unchecked except <u>1. Landlord</u>; likewise the lease summary is blank.

3. Click on <u>2. Property</u>. Select the property the lease is for—if it's not listed, you'll need to add the property, following the on-screen instructions.

At this point, the steps involved in creating this lease are the same as for creating your first *LeaseWriter* lease. For details, see Section B, *Using the Lease Interview to Create a Lease,* above.

3. Using QuickCreate to Create Additional Leases

If you selected QuickCreate, you'll go to the Select Property section of the QuickCreate screen.

Select the address of the property the lease is for—if it's not listed, you'll need to add the property, following the on-screen instructions.

At this point, the steps involved in creating this lease are the same using QuickCreate. For details, see Section C, *Creating a Lease With QuickCreate,* above.

4. Some Data May Already Have Been Entered

The *LeaseWriter* program is actually a set of related databases into which you enter a wide range of information about your rental properties. Data that you enter once on a particular screen may be used many times, in other sections and documents, without you having to enter it again. *LeaseWriter* "knows" when and where to incorporate previously entered information into your documents.

EXAMPLE 1: *Lester Hawkins wants to create a new lease for Apt. C of his building at 1785 Townsend Ave. He's already created a* LeaseWriter *lease for Apt. B at the same address. He goes to the Lease Interview section, clicks on* 2. Property *to select the unit, and enters the required data for this section of the Interview. When he returns to the Lease Interview Menu screen, he sees a check mark next to* 6. Access, Repairs & General Policies. *This is because* LeaseWriter *"assumes" that the general policies in this section (who pays for utilities, etc.) are the same for all units in the same building.*

EXAMPLE 2: *Lester now wants to create a new lease for Apt. D of his building at 1785 Townsend Ave. Since he's already created several* LeaseWriter *leases for units at this address, he goes to the QuickCreate section and selects the unit. When he goes to the General Policies section, most of the data fields are already filled in. This is because* LeaseWriter *"assumes" that the general policies in this section (who pays for utilities, etc.) are the same for all units in the same building.*

EXAMPLE 3: *Lester's wife, Billie, inherits some rental property. When she creates her first* LeaseWriter *lease, she goes to the Lease Interview section, clicks on* 1. Landlord *and enters her name. When she returns to the Lease Interview—Menu Screen, only Part 1 is checked. After she selects* 2. Property, *and enters the required data for this section of the Interview, only Part 2 is checked. No information is carried over from previous leases if the new lease is for a new landlord and a new property.*

Before you print out your document, we advise you look over each interview part (whether checked or not) and data entry field (whether empty or not)—in order to:
- confirm that any information that has already been entered is correct, and
- add any information that has not been entered but is needed.

H. Using Blank Lease Forms

Blank Lead Paint Hazard Disclosure forms and Addendum to Florida Leases can also be accessed in the Create or Change a Lease section of the program. For more on creating these *LeaseWriter* documents, see Chapter 7, *Creating Additional Forms and Letters.*

To access *LeaseWriter's* blank lease forms:
1. Click on the **Main Menu** button in the *LeaseWriter* button bar.
2. Click the **Create or Change a Lease** icon on the left of the screen.
3. Click <u>Blank Lease Forms</u> to go the Blank Lease & Rental Agreement Forms screen.
4. Click on the underlined name of the document you want to open.

Blank forms are print-only forms. *You cannot fill in the Lead Paint Hazard Disclosure or Addendum to Florida Lease using your computer; you'll need to fill in the blanks by hand. This is true of the lease and rental agreement forms listed here as well. If you want to create a custom lease by filling in information on your computer, go to the Create a Lease section of the program, as described above— do not use the blank forms on this screen.*

To preview and print a blank lease form:

1. Open the document, as described above, to open the Document Preview window. The first page of the document is shown.
   - Use the scroll bar to view the entire page.
   - To view the next page, click on the bottom page of the **Notebook** icon in the upper left corner.
   - To return to a previous page, click on the top page of the **Notebook** icon in the upper left corner.
2. To print out a blank copy of the form, click the **Continue** button in the middle of the left side of the screen.
3. At the dialog box that opens, click **Print**.
4. At the Print Setup (Windows) or Page Setup (Macintosh) dialog box, check to make sure the settings are correct, and make any necessary changes. When done, click **OK**.
5. At the Print dialog box that opens, click **Print**.

1. Printing Lead Disclosure Forms in Lease Interview

Since this form should be attached to your lease, we've made it easy to print out the documents together. Here's how:

1. Follow the instructions in Section E to get to the Lease Interview Print/Display screen.
2. Click <u>Preview/Print Lead Disclosure</u>.
3. To print out a blank copy of the form, click the **Continue** button in the middle of the left side of the screen.
4. At the dialog box that opens, click **Print**.
5. At the Print Setup (Windows) or Page Setup (Macintosh) dialog box, check to make sure the settings are correct, and make any necessary changes. When done, click **OK**.
6. At the Print dialog box that opens, click **Print**.

2. Printing Lead Paint Hazard Disclosure Form in QuickCreate

Since a lead disclosure form should be attached to your lease, we've made it easy to print out the documents together. Here's how:

1. Follow the instructions in Section E to get to the QuickCreate Print/Display screen.
2. Click <u>Preview/Print Lead Disclosure</u>.
3. To print out a blank copy of the form, click the **Continue** button in the middle of the left side of the screen.
4. At the dialog box that opens, click **Print**.
5. At the Print Setup (Windows) or Page Setup (Macintosh) dialog box, check to make sure the settings are correct, and make any necessary changes. When done, click **OK**.
6. At the Print dialog box that opens, click **Print**. ■

CHAPTER

7

Creating Additional Forms and Letters

I n addition to the leases and rental agreements (Chapter 6), *LeaseWriter* contains several forms and letters to help you take care of your rental property. The Forms & Letters section includes forms for screening tenants, beginning and ending tenancies, handling repair requests, returning security deposits, etc. The documents in this section are shorter and simpler than the lease and rental agreements discussed in Chapter 6. Accordingly, the process of completing and printing these documents is shorter and simpler as well.

To go to the Forms & Letters section:

1. Click on the **Main Menu** button in the *LeaseWriter* button bar.

2. At the Main Menu screen, click the **Forms & Letters** icon.

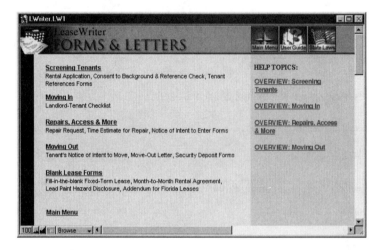

Sections A and B of this chapter discuss some general issues related to the Forms & Letters section. The remainder of the chapter provides more specific information on a section-by-section, form-by-form basis.

A. Documents Included in the Forms & Letters Section

As shown in the above illustration, the left side of the Forms & Letters Menu screen lists its five subsections. Use those lists to (1) locate which subsection a form is in, and (2) go to the corresponding menu screen for that subsection.

FORMS & LETTERS	
Subsections	**Names of Forms**
Screening Tenants	Rental Application
	Consent to Background & Reference Check
	Tenant References Form
Moving In	Landlord-Tenant Checklist
Repairs, Access & More	Resident's Maintenance/Repair Request
	Time Estimate for Repair
	Notice of Intent to Enter Dwelling Unit
Moving Out	Tenant's Notice of Intent to Move
	Move-Out Letter
	Return Entire Security Deposit Form
	Security Deposit Itemization Form
Blank Lease Forms	Fixed-Term Lease
	Month-to-Month Rental Agreement
	Lead Paint Hazard Disclosure Form
	Florida Lease Addendum

These forms and letters have a variety of different characteristics. Some are print only; others can be filled in with your computer. On some forms, you enter information directly into a template that resembles the completed form; other forms are assembled after you enter information (like the leases discussed in Chapter 6).

Section B describes some of these characteristics. Sections C-G contain specific instructions on how to use each form in the Forms & Letters section.

B. Using the Forms & Letters Section

In this section, we explain some of the features you'll encounter as you use the Forms & Letters section of *LeaseWriter*.

1. Why You Can't Fill In the Entire Form With Your Computer

Several forms have blank lines that you can't enter your information into. Here's why:

- The form may need to be given to your tenant or someone else to complete. For example, the Rental Application form should be given to the applicant to complete and return to you. While you need to enter some information, most of the blank fields are for the applicant to fill in.

- The form may need to be filled in by you when away from your computer—for example, the Landlord-Tenant Checklist should be completed while you and your tenant are inspecting the rental unit at move-in or move-out time.

If you're not sure as to why the fields in a particular form are not editable, see the Help Topic for that form for an explanation of its purpose and use.

2. Editing Fields That Already Have Information in Them

Some of the data entry screens in this section include fields that already have information—for example, your name or the address of the unit—filled in when you come to a screen for the first time. This is information which you entered previously in another section of *LeaseWriter* (Rental Property Information or Create or Change a Lease). Sometimes you'll be able to edit this data, other times not. Editable information is in fields, or boxes, with white backgrounds. Information that can't be edited has a gray background, just like the on-screen instructions.

When you edit information in the Forms & Letters section that was previously entered in the Rental Property Information or Create or Change a Lease sections, the edited information is not changed in the part of the program where it was originally entered. Therefore, the edited information will not be accessible in other *LeaseWriter* sections or documents—only to the specific form or letter that's being edited.

If you want to add or modify information so that it will be accessible to other sections and documents in the program, you'll need to: (1) leave the Forms & Letters section; (2) use the Main Menu to find the section where you can add or modify this information; and (3) make the revisions as needed.

3. Adding a Property to a List by Setting It Up

On some of the forms and letters in this section, there's a way of selecting from a list of previously entered addresses, so you won't need to retype. For example, at the top of the Rental Application form, there's a "select address" list of your properties.

If the property you want to create a document for is not listed, it's because you have not completed "setting up" this property by entering it in the Rental Property Information section of the program. While you could just type in the unlisted address, this may not always be the best method.

Why? Because if you just type the address in for a particular form, that property information won't be accessible when you try and create other *LeaseWriter* forms and letters. So if the property you want to create a document for does not show up on such a list *and* you intend to create other *LeaseWriter* documents for that property, you should leave the current document creation screen and add this property to the list. Here's how:

1. Click the **Main Menu** icon in the upper right of the current program window.
2. At the Main Menu screen, click the **Rental Property Information** icon.
3. At the Rental Property Information menu screen, click Set Up Rental Properties.
4. Follow the instruction on screen on how to add properties.
5. When you're done adding the property, use the Main Menu to return to the document you want to create in the Forms & Letters section of the program. When you return to the data entry screen for that document, the property address you just added will be listed in the "select address" box.

For more information on setting up property, see Chapter 5.

4. Blank Lines That Appear When You Add an Item to a List

Throughout the program, you'll see lists—lists of your rental properties, lists of tenants renting a particular unit, lists of cleaning costs deducted from a returned security deposit, and the like. Sometimes you'll see a list that's compiled from information you entered in another part of the program. At other times, you'll be asked to add to the list or modify its items. Whenever you see such a list, you'll also see specific instructions on how to use it.

Most of the lines in a list have several fields for entering data. For example. on the list of properties, each line has fields for address, city, state, zip code and number of units.

As soon as you complete one field and begin typing in another blank field on the same line, a new blank line is created immediately below it. Ignore the new blank line until you want to start typing in it. Then, just click in it to begin. Once again, completing the first field creates a new blank line immediately below the current one.

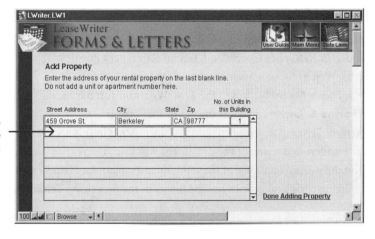

A new blank line is created below the line you're typing in

5. *LeaseWriter's* Document Preview Window

Like the lease documents discussed in Chapter 6, some of the forms in this section are "assembled" after you enter the required information. Before you can print such a form, you must first display it in the Document Preview window.

LeaseWriter's document preview is WYSIWYG—what you see is what you get. You cannot change the font type, font size, or do any kind of reformatting to change how your document will look when it is displayed or printed.

While your document is displayed, you can view each page but cannot do any editing.

A screen shot of *LeaseWriter's* Document Preview Window can be found in Chapter 6, Section E.

- To move around each page of the displayed document, use the scroll bar.
- To move to the next page, click the bottom page of the **Notebook** icon in the upper left of the Document Preview window.
- To go back to a previous page, click the top page of the **Notebook** icon in the upper left of the Document Preview window.
- If you're satisfied with your document and want to print it out, (1) click the **Continue** button on the left of the Document Preview window, (2) in the dialog box that opens, click **Print**, (3) in the Print or Page Setup dialog box, check to make sure the settings are correct, make any necessary changes, and when done click **OK**, (4) in the Print dialog box that opens, click **Print**.
- If you want to revise your document by changing information you entered to create it, (1) click the **Continue** button on the left of the Document Preview window, (2) click **Close** to return to the form's data-entry screen, and (3) make whatever revisions are necessary.

C. Screening Tenants

The following forms can be accessed in this section of the program: Rental Application; Consent to Background & Reference Check; and Tenant References Form.

To create LeaseWriter documents for screening tenants:

1. Click on the **Main Menu** button in the *LeaseWriter* button bar.
2. Click the **Forms & Letters** icon on the left of the screen.
3. Click Screening Tenants to see a listing of the documents in this section.
4. Click on the underlined name of the document you want to create.

For details on the purpose and use of these documents, read the Help Topics for this part of the program. Instructions on how to use the forms in the Screening Tenants section are given below.

1. Rental Application

This document is to be given to prospective tenants to apply for a vacancy. For details on the purpose and use of this document, read the Help Topics for this part of the program.

a. Opening the Document

To open the Rental Application form:

1. Click on the **Main Menu** button in the *LeaseWriter* button bar.
2. At the Main Menu screen, click the **Forms & Letters** icon on the left of the screen.
3. At the Forms & Letters Menu screen, click Screening Tenants.
4. At the Screening Tenants Menu screen, click Rental Application.

b. Filling In the Document

For information on using this document, click on the help topic How to Use the Rental Application form.

Follow the instructions on screen on what information you need to enter for this document. Note that you will only be able to fill in the upper portion; most of the displayed form contains blank lines that you can't enter information into. These lines are for the applicant to fill in.

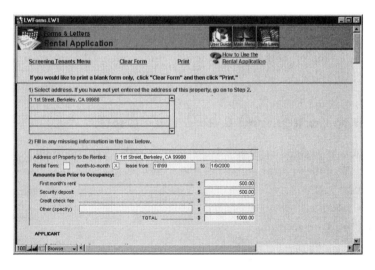

Fill in the address of the property the application is for. If you previously "set up" the property the application is for (see Chapter 5), you'll be able to select the address from the "select address" list box. If the property the application is for is not listed in the "select address" list box, you can either:

- type it in the space indicated, or
- leave the current document creation screen and add this property to the list by setting it up in the Rental Property Information section of *LeaseWriter*. See Section B3, *Adding a Property to a List by Setting It Up*, above.

c. Printing the Document

To print the Rental Application form:
1. Open and fill in the document, as described above.
2. At the top of the Rental Application screen, click <u>Print</u>.
3. This opens a standard Print or Page Setup dialog box. Check to make sure the settings are correct, and make any necessary changes. When done, click **OK**.
4. This opens a standard Print dialog box. If you want to print out more than one copy, enter the number you want.
5. Click **OK**.

To print a blank version of the form, click <u>Clear Form</u> at the top of the Rental Application screen. While doing this "empties" all the fields on your screen, it does not delete information entered previously in other sections of *LeaseWriter*. Then, follow Steps 2-5, above.

d. When You're Done

To leave the Rental Application form and go to another document in the Forms & Letters section:
1. Click <u>Screening Tenants Menu</u> at the upper left of the current document window.
2. Use the list on the left of the screen to select another related document or return to the <u>Forms & Letters Menu</u>.

2. Consent to Background & Reference Check

This document is to be given to prospective tenants. It authorizes you to check their references. For details on the purpose and use of this document, read the Help Topics for this part of the program.

a. Opening the Document

To open the Consent to Background & Reference Check form:
1. Click on the **Main Menu** button in the *LeaseWriter* button bar.
2. At the Main Menu screen, click the **Forms & Letters** icon on the left of the screen.
3. At the Forms & Letters Menu screen, click <u>Screening Tenants</u>.
4. At the Screening Tenants Menu screen, click <u>Consent to Background & Reference Check</u>.

b. Filling In the Document

For information on using this document, click on the Help Topic <u>How to Use the Consent to Background & Reference Check Form</u>.

Follow the instructions on screen on what information you need to enter for this document. In this case, your name is the only required information, and it is inserted automatically. Note that you will only be able to fill in the upper portion; most of this form has blank lines that you can't enter information into. These lines are for the applicant to fill in.

c. Printing the Document

To print the Consent to Background & Reference Check form:
1. Open and fill in the document, as described above.
2. At the top of the Consent to Background & Reference Check screen, click <u>Print</u>.
3. This opens a standard Print Setup (Windows) or Page Setup (Macintosh) dialog box. Check to make sure the settings are correct, and make any necessary changes. When done, click **OK**.
4. This opens a standard Print dialog box. If you want to print out more than one copy, enter the number you want.
5. Click **OK**.

To print a blank version of the form, click <u>Clear Form</u> at the top of the Consent to Background and Reference Check screen. While doing this "empties" all the fields on your screen, it does not delete information entered previously in other sections of *LeaseWriter*. Then, follow Steps 2-5, above.

d. When You're Done

To leave the Consent to Background & Reference Check form and go to another document in the Forms & Letters section:
1. Click <u>Screening Tenants Menu</u> at the upper left of the current document window.
2. Use the list on the left of the screen to select another related document or return to the <u>Forms & Letters Menu</u>.

3. Tenant References Form

This document is used to keep track of your conversations with a prospective tenant's references. For details on the purpose and use of this document, read the Help Topics for this part of the program.

a. Opening the Document

To open the Tenant References form:
1. Click on the **Main Menu** button in the *LeaseWriter* button bar.
2. At the Main Menu screen, click the **Forms & Letters** icon on the left of the screen.
3. At the Forms & Letters Menu screen, click Screening Tenants.
4. At the Screening Tenants Menu screen, click Tenant References.

b. Filling In the Document

For information on using this document, click on the help topic How to Use the Tenant References Form.

Follow the instructions on screen on what information you need to enter for this document. Note that you will only be able to fill in the upper portion; most of this form has blank lines that you can't enter information into. You will be completing this form by hand after you talk to the prospective tenant's references.

You must fill in the address of the property the form is for. If you previously "set up" the property the form is for (see Chapter 5), you'll be able to select the address from the "select address" list box. If the property the form is for is for is not listed in the "select address" list box, you can either:
- type it in the space indicated, or
- leave the current document creation screen and add this property to the list by setting it up in the Rental Property Information section of *LeaseWriter*. See Section B3, *Adding a Property to a List by Setting It Up*, above.

c. Printing the Document

To print the Tenant References form:
1. Open and fill in the document, as described above.
2. At the top of the Tenant References screen, click Print.
3. This opens a standard Print Setup (Windows) or Page Setup (Macintosh) dialog box. Check to make sure the settings are correct, and make any necessary changes. When done, click **OK**.
4. This opens a standard Print dialog box. If you want to print out more than one copy, enter the number you want.
5. Click **OK**.

To print a blank version of the form, click Clear Form at the top of the Tenant References screen. While doing this "empties" all the fields on your screen, it does not delete information entered previously in other sections of *LeaseWriter*. Then, follow Steps 2-5, above.

d. When You're Done

To leave the Tenant References form and go to another document in the Forms & Letters section:
1. Click <u>Screening Tenants Menu</u> at the upper left of the current document window.
2. Use the list on the left of the screen to select another related document or return to the <u>Forms & Letters Menu</u>.

D. Moving In: The Landlord-Tenant Checklist

The Landlord-Tenant Checklist is the only form in this section of the program. This document is to be filled in by hand as you inspect the premises before your tenant moves in, and again at move-out time. For details on the purpose and use of this document, read the Help Topics for this part of the program.

a. Opening the Document

To open the Landlord-Tenant Checklist form:
1. Click on the **Main Menu** button in the *LeaseWriter* button bar.
2. At the Main Menu screen, click the **Forms & Letters** icon on the left of the screen.
3. At the Forms & Letters Menu screen, click <u>Moving In</u>.
4. At the Moving In Menu screen, click <u>Landlord-Tenant Checklist</u>.

> **This is a print-only form.** *Because the Landlord-Tenant Checklist should be filled in by hand while you and your tenant are touring the rental unit, you cannot fill it in using your computer.*

b. Previewing and Printing the Document

To preview and print the Landlord-Tenant Checklist form:
1. Open the document, as described above, to open the Document Preview window. The first page of the document is shown.
   - Use the scroll bar to view the entire page.
   - To view the next page, click on the bottom "page" of the **Notebook** icon in the upper left corner.
   - To return to a previous page, click on the top "page" of the **Notebook** icon in the upper left corner.
2. To print out a blank copy of the form, click the **Continue** button in the middle of the left side of the screen.
3. At the dialog box that opens, click **Print**.

4. At the Print Setup (Windows) or Page Setup (Macintosh) dialog box, check to make sure the settings are correct, and make any necessary changes. When done, click **OK**.

5. At the Print dialog box that opens, click **Print**.

For more on using *LeaseWriter*'s Document Preview window, see Section B5, above.

c. When You're Done

To leave the Landlord-Tenant Checklist and go to another document in the Forms & Letter section, click Forms & Letters Menu at the bottom of the Moving In Menu screen.

E. Repairs, Access & More

The following forms are included in this section of the program: Resident's Maintenance/ Repair Request; Time Estimate for Repair; and Notice of Intent to Enter Dwelling Unit.

To create any of these *LeaseWriter* documents:

1. Click on the **Main Menu** button in the *LeaseWriter* button bar.

2. Click the **Forms & Letters** icon on the left of the screen.

3. Click Repairs, Access & More to see a listing of the documents in this section.

4. Click on the underlined name of the document you want to create.

For details on the purpose and use of this document, read the Help Topics for this part of the program. Instructions on how to use the forms in the Repairs, Access & More section are given below.

1. Resident's Maintenance/Repair Request Form

This document is for your tenant's use in requesting repairs. For details on the purpose and use of this document, read the Help Topics for this part of the program.

a. Opening the Document

To open the Resident's Maintenance/Repair Request form:

1. Click on the **Main Menu** button in the *LeaseWriter* button bar.

2. At the Main Menu screen, click the **Forms & Letters** icon on the left of the screen.

3. At the Forms & Letters Menu screen, click Repairs, Access & More.

4. At the Repairs, Access & More Menu screen, click Resident's Maintenance/Repair Request.

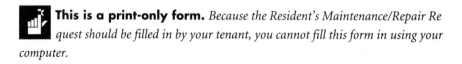 **This is a print-only form.** *Because the Resident's Maintenance/Repair Request should be filled in by your tenant, you cannot fill this form in using your computer.*

b. Printing the Document

To print a Resident's Maintenance/Repair Request Form:
1. Open the document, as described above.
2. At the top of the Resident's Maintenance/Repair Request Form screen, click Print.
3. This opens a standard Print Setup (Windows) or Page Setup (Macintosh) dialog box. Check to make sure the settings are correct, and make any necessary changes. When done, click **OK**.
4. This opens a standard Print dialog box. If you want to print out more than one copy (a good idea, to ensure that your tenants will always have a copy on hand), enter the number you want.
5. Click **OK**.

c. When You're Done

To leave the Resident's Maintenance/Repair Request Form and go to another document in the Forms & Letters section:
1. Click Repairs & Access Menu at the upper left of the current document window.
2. Use the list on the left of the screen to select another related document or return to the Forms & Letters Menu.

2. Time Estimate for Repair

This document is to used to respond to a tenant's request for maintenance or repair. For details on the purpose and use of this document, read the Help Topics for this part of the program.

a. Opening the Document

To open the Time Estimate for Repair form:
1. Click on the **Main Menu** button in the *LeaseWriter* button bar.
2. At the Main Menu screen, click the **Forms & Letters** icon on the left of the screen.
3. At the Forms & Letters Menu screen, click Repairs, Access & More.
4. At the Repairs, Access & More Menu screen, click Time Estimate for Repair.

b. Filling in the Document

For information on using this document, click on the help topic How to Use the Time Estimate for Repair Form.

Follow the instructions on screen on what information you need to enter for this document. When you first open the form, all fields are blank. This is because none of the data you entered previously into *LeaseWriter* are used in this document.

c. Printing the Document

To print the Time Estimate for Repair form:
1. Open and fill in the document, as described above.
2. At the top of the Time Estimate for Repair screen, click <u>Print</u>.
3. This opens a standard Print Setup (Windows) or Page Setup (Macintosh) dialog box. Check to make sure the settings are correct, and make any necessary changes. When done, click **OK**.
4. This opens a standard Print dialog box. If you want to print out more than one copy, enter the number you want.
5. Click **OK**.

To print a blank version of the form, click <u>Clear Form</u> at the top of the Time Estimate for Repair screen. While doing this "empties" all the fields on your screen, it does not delete information entered previously in other sections of *LeaseWriter*. Then, follow Steps 2-5, above.

d. When You're Done

To leave the Time Estimate for Repair Form and go to another document in the Forms & Letters section:
1. Click <u>Repairs, Access & More</u> at the upper left of the current document window.
2. Use the list on the left of the screen to select another related document or return to the <u>Forms & Letters Menu</u>.

3. Notice of Intent to Enter Dwelling Unit

This document is used to notify your tenant before you enter their unit. For details on the purpose and use of this document, read the Help Topics for this part of the program.

a. Opening the Document

To open the Notice of Intent to Enter Dwelling Unit form:
1. Click on the **Main Menu** button in the *LeaseWriter* button bar.
2. At the Main Menu screen, click the **Forms & Letters** icon on the left of the screen.
3. At the Forms & Letters Menu screen, click <u>Repairs, Access & More</u>.
4. At the Repairs, Access & More Menu screen, click <u>Notice of Intent to Enter Dwelling Unit</u>.

b. Filling In the Document

For information on using this document, click on the Help Topic <u>How to Use the Notice of Intent to Enter Dwelling Unit Form</u>.

Follow the instructions on screen on what information you need to enter for this document. Note that when you first open the form, all fields are blank. This is because none of the data you entered previously into *LeaseWriter* are used in this document.

c. Printing the Document

To print the Notice of Intent to Enter Dwelling Unit form:

1. Open and fill in the document, as described above.
2. At the top of the Notice of Intent to Enter Dwelling Unit screen, click **Print**.
3. This opens a standard Print Setup (Windows) or Page Setup (Macintosh) dialog box. Check to make sure the settings are correct, and make any necessary changes. When done, click **OK**.
4. This opens a standard Print dialog box. If you want to print out more than one copy, enter the number you want.
5. Click **OK**.

To print a blank version of the form, click <u>Clear Form</u> at the top of the Notice of Intent to Enter Dwelling Unit screen. While doing this "empties" all the fields on your screen, it does not delete information entered previously in other sections of *LeaseWriter*. Then, follow Steps 2-5, above.

d. When You're Done

To leave the Notice of Intent to Enter Dwelling Unit form and go to another document in the Forms & Letters section:

1. Click <u>Repairs & Access Menu</u> at the upper left of the current document window.
2. Use the list on the left of the screen to select another related document or return to the <u>Forms & Letters Menu</u>.

F. Moving Out

The following forms are included in this section of the program: Tenant's Notice of Intent to Move Out; Move-Out Letter; Return Entire Security Deposit Forms; and Security Deposit Itemization Form.

To create *LeaseWriter* documents for use when tenants move out:

1. Click on the **Main Menu** button in the *LeaseWriter* button bar.
2. Click the **Forms & Letters** icon on the left of the screen.
3. Click <u>Moving Out</u> to see a listing of the documents in this section.
4. Click on the underlined name of the document you want to create.

For details on the purpose and use of these documents, read the Help Topics for this part of the program. Instructions on how to use the forms in the Moving Out section are given below.

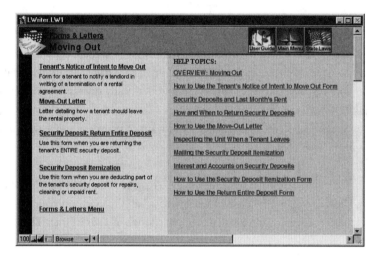

1. Tenant's Notice of Intent to Move Out

This document is given to tenants to fill out by hand to notify you that they are ending their tenancy. For details on the purpose and use of this document, read the Help Topics for this part of the program.

a. Opening the Document

To open the Tenant's Notice of Intent to Move Out form:

1. Click on the **Main Menu** button in the *LeaseWriter* button bar.
2. At the Main Menu screen, click the **Forms & Letters** icon on the left of the screen.
3. At the Forms & Letters Menu screen, click <u>Moving Out</u>.
4. At the Screening Tenants Menu screen, click <u>Tenant's Notice of Intent to Move Out</u>.

b. Filling In the Document

For information on using this document, click on the help topic <u>How to Use the Tenant's Notice of Intent to Move Out Form</u>.

Follow the instructions on screen on what information you need to enter for this document. Note that you will only be able to fill in your name and address and the address of the rental unit. Most of this form has blank lines that you can't enter information into—they need to be filled in by your tenant before returning the form to you.

c. Printing the Document

To print the Tenant's Notice of Intent to Move Out form:
1. Open and fill in the document, as described above.
2. At the top of the Tenant's Notice of Intent to Move Out screen, click <u>Print</u>.
3. This opens a standard Print Setup (Windows) or Page Setup (Macintosh) dialog box. Check to make sure the settings are correct, and make any necessary changes. When done, click **OK**.
4. This opens a standard Print dialog box. If you want to print out more than one copy, enter the number you want.
5. Click **OK**.

To print a blank version of the form, click <u>Clear Form</u> at the top of the Tenant References screen. While doing this "empties" all the fields on your screen, it does not delete information entered previously in other sections of *LeaseWriter*. Then, follow Steps 2-5, above.

d. When You're Done

To leave the Tenant's Notice of Intent to Move Out form and go to another document in the Moving Out section:
1. Click <u>Moving Out Menu</u> at the upper left of the current document window.
2. Use the list on the left of the screen to select another related document or return to the <u>Forms & Letters Menu</u>.

2. Move-Out Letter

This document is to be given to tenants, informing them what they must do before ending their tenancy. For details on the purpose and use of this document, read the Help Topics for this part of the program.

a. Opening the Document

To open the Move-Out Letter form:
1. Click on the **Main Menu** button in the *LeaseWriter* button bar.
2. At the Main Menu screen, click the **Forms & Letters** icon on the left of the screen.
3. At the Forms & Letters Menu screen, click <u>Moving Out</u>.
4. At the Screening Tenants Menu screen, click <u>Move-Out Letter</u>.

b. Filling In the Document

For information on using this document, click on the help topic <u>How to Use the Move-Out Letter</u>.

Follow the instructions on screen on what information you need to enter to complete this document. Because this form works differently than the others found in this part of *LeaseWriter*, we suggest you carefully read the remainder of this section. For details on re-storing the original default text after you've created and edited a move-out letter, see *Creating Additional Move-Out Letters*, below.

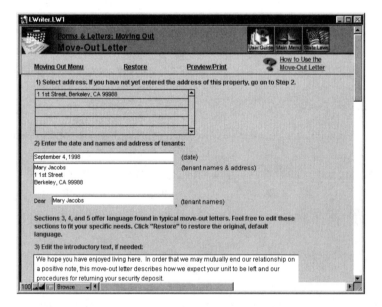

STEP 1

You must fill in the address of the property the Move-Out letter is for. If you previously "set up" the property the Letter is for (see Chapter 5), you'll be able to select the address from the "select address" list box by clicking on it. If the Letter is for property that is not listed in the "select address" list box, you can either:

- type the address in the space indicated (see Step 2, below), or
- leave the current document creation screen and add this property to the list by setting it up in the Rental Property Information section of *LeaseWriter*. See Section B3, *Adding a Property to a List by Setting It Up*, above.

STEP 2

The date is entered automatically, but you can change it if you wish. For details on how to restore the default text after you make changes, see *Creating Additional Move-Out Letters*, below.

    If you made a selection in Step 1, your tenant's name and address will be filled in automatically. If not, fill it in.

 **Why the tenant name field is blank.** *If you did not previously record the tenant's name when you "set up" this property (see Chapter 5), the field will remain blank after you make the selection in Step 1.*

STEP 3

You can customize the introductory text, or just leave it as is. Just edit as you would using your word processor; if you want you can use the standard editing commands in *LeaseWriter*'s Edit menu. For details on how to restore the default text after you make changes, see *Creating Additional Move-Out Letters*, below.

STEP 4

Follow the on-screen instructions to list the items you want the tenant to clean before moving out. You're limited to twenty lines. Just edit as you would using your word processor; if you want you can use the standard editing commands in the Edit menu in *LeaseWriter*'s menu bar. For details on how to restore the default text after you make changes, see *Creating Additional Move-Out Letters*, below.

STEP 5

Fill in the blanks with the appropriate information. Just edit as you would using your word processor; if you want you can use the standard editing commands in *LeaseWriter*'s Edit menu. If you want you can make other changes to the concluding text, or just leave it as is. For details on how to restore the default text after you make changes, see *Creating Additional Move-Out Letters*, below.

c. Printing the Document

To print the Move-Out Letter:

1. Open and fill in the document, as described above.
2. At the top of the Move-Out Letter screen, click <u>Preview/Print</u> to open the Document Preview window. The first page of your document is shown.
   - Use the scroll bar to view the entire page.
   - To view the next page, click on the bottom page of the **Notebook** icon in the upper left corner.
   - To return to a previous page, click on the top page of the **Notebook** icon in the upper left corner.
3. To print out a blank copy of the form, click the **Continue** button in the middle of the left side of the screen.
4. At the dialog box that opens, click **Print**.
5. This opens a standard Print Setup (Windows) or Page Setup (Macintosh) dialog box. Check to make sure the settings are correct, and make any necessary changes. When done, click **OK**.
6. At the Print dialog box that opens, click **Print**.

   For more on using *LeaseWriter*'s Document Preview window, see Section B5.

d. When You're Done

To leave the Move-Out Letter form and go to another document in the Moving-Out section:

1. Click <u>Moving-Out Menu</u> at the upper left of the current document window.
2. Use the list on the left of the screen to select another related document or return to the <u>Forms & Letters Menu</u>.

e. Creating Additional Move-Out Letters

Any editing you do will "replace" the default language you saw the first time you came to the screen for this form. Is this a problem if you want to customize the language to fit the specific rental unit each time you fill in the form?

Don't worry. You can always restore the original text by clicking <u>Restore</u> at the top of the Move-Out Letter screen. Be aware that if you do this, it deletes all your changes, including those that you might want to include in *all* your move-out letters (like your phone number or your security deposit return policy).

> **EXAMPLE:** *Lester Hawkins creates a Move-Out Letter for his tenants in Apt. C, filling in required information and requesting that his tenants clean out the garage and fireplace. Four months later, his tenant in Apt. B informs him that she's moving as well. Lester uses LeaseWriter's menus to go to the Move-Out Letter screen. When he does, he sees the text for the letter he wrote for Apt. C. Lester wants to change some of the text, to include his new phone number and delete the requirement that the garage be cleaned (since this tenant didn't rent a garage). Rather than restore the original text and begin re-editing from scratch, he simply deletes the line in Step 4 about cleaning the garage and revises his phone number in Step 5.*

3. Security Deposit: Return Entire Deposit

This document is to be given to tenants when you are returning their entire security deposit. For details on the purpose and use of this document, read the Help Topics for this part of the program.

a. Opening the Document

To open the Security Deposit: Return Entire Deposit form:
1. Click on the **Main Menu** button in the *LeaseWriter* button bar.
2. At the Main Menu screen, click the **Forms & Letters** icon on the left of the screen.
3. At the Forms & Letters Menu screen, click <u>Moving Out</u>.
4. At the Screening Tenants Menu screen, click <u>Security Deposit: Return Entire Deposit</u>.

b. Filling In the Document

For information on using this document, click on the Help Topics <u>How and When to Return Security Deposits</u> and <u>How to Use the Return Entire Deposit Form</u>.

Follow the instructions on screen on what information you need to enter to complete this document. The sequence of screens and the information you'll be prompted to enter varies from user to user, depending what information has been previously entered into *LeaseWriter* about the property this document is for.

The Choose Lease and Select Unit Screens

The names and order of the screens you'll see next depend on whether the property and/or unit you are returning the security deposit for:

- has been set up in *LeaseWriter*'s Property Information section
- has a *LeaseWriter* lease
- has other relevant information about it entered into *LeaseWriter*.

You needn't worry about which scenario is being played out—*LeaseWriter* will ask you to enter whatever information it needs to know. Just carefully read and follow the on-screen instructions.

When you've entered the required information and selected the unit this document is for, you'll go to a screen where you enter specific information for this document. For further instructions, see *Enter Specific Information*, below.

Enter Specific Information

Follow the instructions on screen to enter the necessary information about the tenancy and the deposit. Notice that some of the fields are already filled in with data you entered previously into *LeaseWriter*.

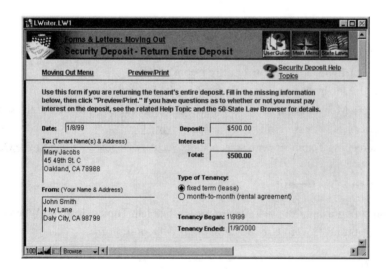

c. Printing the Document

To print the Security Deposit: Return Entire Deposit form:
1. Open and fill in the document, as described above.
2. At the top of the Return Entire Security Deposit screen, click <u>Preview/Print</u> to open the Document Preview window. The first page of your document is shown.
    • Use the scroll bar to view the entire page.
    • To view the next page, click on the bottom page of the **Notebook** icon in the upper left corner.
    • To return to a previous page, click on the top page of the **Notebook** icon in the upper left corner.
3. To print out a blank copy of the form, click the **Continue** button in the middle of the left side of the screen.
4. At the dialog box that opens, click **Print**.
5. This opens a standard Print Setup (Windows) or Page Setup (Macintosh) dialog box. Check to make sure the settings are correct, and make any necessary changes. When done, click **OK**.
6. At the Print dialog box that opens, click **Print**.
    For more on using *LeaseWriter*'s Document Preview window, see Section B5, above.

d. When You're Done

To leave the Security Deposit: Return Entire Deposit form and go to another document in the Moving Out section:
1. Click <u>Moving Out Menu</u> at the upper left of the current document window.
2. Use the list on the left of the screen to select another related document or return to the <u>Forms & Letters Menu</u>.

4. Security Deposit Itemization Form

This document is to be given to tenants when you are returning only a portion of their security deposit. For details on the purpose and use of this document, read the Help Topics for this part of the program.

a. Opening the Document

To open the Security Deposit Itemization form:
1. Click on the **Main Menu** button in the *LeaseWriter* button bar.
2. At the Main Menu screen, click the **Forms & Letters** icon on the left of the screen.
3. At the Forms & Letters Menu screen, click Moving Out.
4. At the Screening Tenants Menu screen, click Security Deposit Itemization.

b. Filling In the Document

For information on using this document, click on the Help Topics *How and When to Return Security Deposits* and *How to Use the Security Deposit Itemization Form.* Follow the instructions on screen on what information you need to enter to complete this document. The sequence of screens and the information you'll be prompted to enter varies from user to user, depending on what information has been previously entered into *LeaseWriter* about the property this document is for.

The Choose Lease and Select Unit screens

The names and order of the screens you'll see next depend on whether the property and/or unit you are returning the security deposit for:
- has been set up in *LeaseWriter*'s Property Information section
- has a *LeaseWriter* lease
- has other relevant information about it entered into *LeaseWriter.*

You needn't worry about which scenario is being played out—*LeaseWriter* will ask you to enter whatever information it needs to know. Just carefully read and follow the on-screen instructions.

When you've entered the required information and selected the unit this document is for, you'll go to a screen where you enter specific information for this document. For further instructions, see *Enter Specific Information,* below.

Enter Specific Information

Follow the instructions on screen to enter the necessary information on three data entry screens. Notice that some of the fields are already filled in, using data you entered previously into *LeaseWriter.*
1. **Address Info** Follow the instructions on screen to enter the required data. When done, click Itemize Deposit at the top of the screen.

2. **Itemize Deposit** Follow the instructions on screen to itemize and explain your deductions. Use the TAB key to move down to the next data entry field. Don't worry about adding all these items up—*LeaseWriter* does that for you. When done, click Total/Comments at the top of the screen.

3. **Total/Comments** If you want to add any comments to this itemization, do so here.

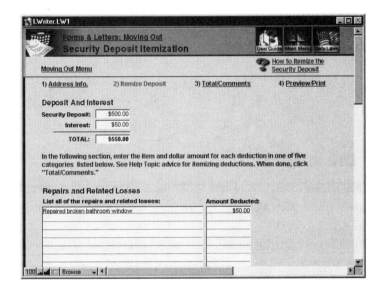

c. Printing the Document

To print the Security Deposit Itemization form:

1. Open and fill in the document, as described above.

2. At the top of the Security Deposit Itemization screen, click Preview/Print to open the Document Preview window. The first page of your document is shown.
   - Use the scroll bar to view the entire page.
   - To view the next page, click on the bottom page of the **Notebook** icon in the upper left corner.
   - To return to a previous page, click on the top page of the **Notebook** icon in the upper left corner.

3. To print out the form, click the **Continue** button in the middle of the left side of the screen.

4. At the dialog box that opens, click **Print**.
5. At the Print Setup (Windows) or Page Setup (Macintosh) dialog box, check to make
   sure the settings are correct, and make any necessary changes. When done, click **OK**.
6. At the Print dialog box that opens, click **Print**.

For more on using *LeaseWriter*'s Document Preview window, see Section B5.

d. When You're Done

To leave the Security Deposit Itemization form and go to another document in the Moving
Out sections:
1. Click <u>Moving Out Menu</u> at the upper left of the current document window.
2. Use the list on the left of the screen to select another related document or return to the
   <u>Forms & Letters Menu</u>.

G. Blank Lease Forms

The following blank lease forms can be accessed in this section of the program: Fixed-Term
Lease, Month-to-Month Rental Agreement, Lead Paint Hazard Disclosure Form, and Addendum to Florida Leases.

   When you click <u>Blank Lease Forms</u> at the Forms & Letters menu screen, you leave the
Forms & Letters section of *LeaseWriter* and go to the Create or Change a Lease section. From
there, you can display and print these forms. For details on how to use *LeaseWriter*'s lease
forms, see Chapter 6, Section H. ■

CHAPTER

8

Troubleshooting

T his section of the manual briefly discusses some common technical difficulties you might encounter in running the *LeaseWriter* program. Remember, help is also available by clicking the **User Guide** icon on the upper right of all *LeaseWriter* screens.

If This Chapter Doesn't Clear Up Your Problem

- If you have questions that are not answered in this section, see also Chapter 3, Section B, *Frequently Asked Questions About LeaseWriter.*
- If you have specific questions about problems with your lease document, see also Chapter 6, Section D, *Tips on Entering Information to Create Leases.*
- If you still haven't solved your problem, contact Nolo Tech Support (see Section F, below).

A. Installing Under Windows

1. Displaying the "Welcome to *LeaseWriter*" Screen

To install *LeaseWriter*, follow the instructions in Chapter 2, Section A. When you insert the *LeaseWriter* CD, the "Welcome to *LeaseWriter*" screen should open automatically. If this does not happen, do the following:

1. Choose Run from the Start menu on your Window taskbar.
2. Click the **Browse** button.
3. Type X:\WELCOME.HLP (substitute the letter of your CD-ROM drive for "X").
4. Click **OK**.

2. Finding the File SETUP.EXE on the *LeaseWriter* CD

The installation program SETUP.EXE is located in the root directory of the CD-ROM. If you want to start this program from the Run command line, enter X:\SETUP (substitute the letter of your CD-ROM drive for "X").

B. Problems With How *LeaseWriter* Appears on Your Screen

1. Windows: Running *LeaseWriter* With Non Standard Display Properties

If you run *LeaseWriter* under 640 x 480 screen resolution *and* are not using standard Windows 95 (or 98) display properties, you may not be able to see all the text and graphics on *LeaseWriter*'s screens without scrolling.

To solve this problem, you need to change to standard display properties. Here's how:
1. Exit *LeaseWriter*.
2. Using your mouse, point anywhere on your PC's desktop and right-click.
3. From the Desktop menu, click Properties. This opens the Display Properties window.
4. Click the **Appearance** tab.
5. Pull down the Scheme: menu and select "Windows Standard."
6. Click **Apply**.
When you restart *LeaseWriter*, it should look fine.

2. Macintosh: If Arial and Helvetica Fonts Are Not installed

LeaseWriter was developed using Arial, one of the most common Windows fonts. While most Macs also have this font (especially those with MicroSoft Word 6 or higher), some don't.

If you don't have Arial, *LeaseWriter* text usually maps to Helvetica, a common Mac font. If you have Helvetica installed, and *LeaseWriter* maps to Helvetica, all *LeaseWriter* screen text should appear as intended.

If for some reason text appears cut off or misaligned, here are two possible solutions:
1. Go to the Fonts folder in your Mac's system folder and make sure that Helvetica is installed and enabled. This will usually clear up the problem.
2. If the problem persists, install the Arial font.
Note that this is just a cosmetic problem and you will be able to use *LeaseWriter* even if Arial and Helvetica are not installed.

C. Printing in *LeaseWriter*

Please read this section if you run into problems printing *LeaseWriter* documents or Help Topics. For specific instructions on how to print in *LeaseWriter*, see also:

- Chapter 4 on printing Help Topics and state rental law summaries
- Chapter 5 on printing rental property summaries
- Chapter 6 on printing lease and rental agreement documents
- Chapter 7 on printing other *LeaseWriter* forms and letters.

1. Printing Assembled Documents From the Document Preview Window

As described in Chapters 5-7, some documents are "assembled" after you enter the required information. *LeaseWriter* then displays them in a Document Preview window. When these forms are displayed, you can print them out.

a. Navigating the Document Preview Window

- To move around each page of the displayed document, use the scroll bar.
- To move to the next page, click the bottom page of the **Notebook** icon in the upper left of the Document Preview window.
- To go back to a previous page, click the top page of the **Notebook** icon in the upper left of the Document Preview window.

⚠ Don't maximize and minimize the Document Preview window.
First maximizing and then minimizing an open Document Preview window can cause the main LeaseWriter *program window to freeze. If this happens, no data will be lost, but you'll need to exit and restart the* LeaseWriter *program. To prevent this, do not maximize or minimize an open Document Preview window.*

b. Changing Your Document Before You Print It

1. Click the **Continue** button on the left of the Document Preview window.
2. Click **Close** to return to the Printing/Displaying the Lease screen.
3. Go to the field where you entered the information you want to change and make your revisions.
4. When done, click <u>Preview/Print</u> to display the revised document.

c. Printing Out the Displayed Document

1. Click the **Continue** button on the left side of the Document Preview window.
2. Click **OK** when you're asked if you want to print the lease.

3. At the Print Setup (Windows) or Page Setup (Macintosh) dialog box, check to make sure the settings are correct, and make any necessary changes. When done, click **OK**.

4. At the Print dialog box that opens, click **Print**.

> ⚠️ **Don't touch the setting in the Print dialog box.**
> LeaseWriter *uses specific settings tailored for each* LeaseWriter *document. There is no need to touch these default settings—in fact doing so could cause problems. While the Print dialog box is open, you should only:*
> * *change the number of copies to be printed, if necessary*
> * *click the* **OK** *or* **Cancel** *buttons.*

2. Formatting *LeaseWriter* Documents

You will not be able to reformat *any LeaseWriter* documents. Font, font size, margins, etc., are all set in advance and should be more than adequate for the simple documents you create using *LeaseWriter*.

3. Printing Multi-Page Help Topics

Sometimes *LeaseWriter* cuts off the bottom line when printing multiple-page topics from Legal Help Topics and the User Guide. If this happens to you, you'll need to reduce the Scaling setting for your printer. Here's how:

a. Windows

1. Display the topic you want to print out (see Chapter 4 on displaying Legal Help Topics and User Guide topics).

2. Click the **Print** button in the upper right of the open Help Topic window. This opens a Print Setup dialog box. Make sure your printer is selected in the Name: field.

3. In the Print Setup dialog box, click the **Properties** button. This opens the Printer Properties dialog box for the selected printer.

4. Click on the **Graphics** tab.

5. Reduce the percentage in the Scaling field by 2—for example, if the default is 100%, change it to 98%. When done, click **OK** to close the Printer Properties dialog box and return to the Print Setup dialog box.

6. Continue the steps for printing.

  After you're done printing *LeaseWriter* Help Topics, go back and restore your printer settings to what they were before you changed them in Step 5, otherwise these settings will be used when you print from other programs as well.

b. Macintosh

1. Display the topic you want to print out (see Chapter 4 on displaying Legal Help Topics and User Guide topics).
2. Click the **Print** button in the upper right of the open Help Topic window. This opens a Page Setup dialog box.
3. In the Print Setup dialog box, reduce the percentage in the Scaling field by 2—for example, if the default is 100%, change it to 98%. When done, click **OK** to close the Printer Properties dialog box and return to the Print Setup dialog box.
4. Continue the steps for printing.

After you're done printing *LeaseWriter* Help Topics, go back and restore your printer settings to what they were before you changed them in Step 3, otherwise these settings will be used when you print from other programs as well.

Copying Text From *LeaseWriter* Help Topics

You can also copy text from *LeaseWriter* Help Topics, and paste it into your word processor or other programs. Here's how:

1. Display the topic you want to print out (see Chapter 4 on displaying Legal Help Topics and User Guide topics).
2. Use your mouse to select all the text you want to copy.
3. Choose Copy from *LeaseWriter*'s Edit menu. This copies the selected text to your computer's clipboard.
4. Switch over to your word processor, and use its Paste command to paste the clipboard's contents into a word processing document.

Now, you can use your word processor's Print command to print it out.

Note that text from other *LeaseWriter* program screens cannot be copied this way—only Legal Help Topics and User Guide topics.

D. Launching Your Web Browser (Windows Users)

As discussed in Chapter 4, Section C, *LeaseWriter*'s 50-State Law Browser contains links to state landlord-tenant statutes on the Internet. To use this feature under Windows, you must have your *default* Web browser already running. (The 50-State Law Browser in *LeaseWriter* for Macintosh will start your browser for you if it's not already running).

Windows users who have more than one browser installed may find that the 50-State Law Browser does not connect them to the sites they click on. This will happen if the browser that is opened is not your *default* browser.

If you find that the 50-State Law Browser is not connecting with the site you click on, you'll need to:

1. Exit the Web browser that's currently running.
2. Start your default browser.
3. Try connecting using the 50-State Law Browser's Web access feature again.

E. Using *LeaseWriter's* Backup Files

As we all know, power failures and hardware problems can happen to anyone, at any time. If this happens when you're running *LeaseWriter*, your files may be damaged and the program may become unusable. If this happens you'll need to: (1) reinstall *LeaseWriter*, and (2) import your data from the backup files you create when you exit the program.

1. Backing Up Your Data When You Exit

When you install *LeaseWriter*, seven backup files are created. Each time you exit, you'll see a dialog box asking if you want to back up your data to these files. Although this process takes 10-15 seconds, we strongly recommend that you back up your data. If you do not export your data to these backup files, you will not have any way to recover your data in case of an unexpected crash.

To create a backup of your data, click the **OK** button when you see the Backup dialog box.

2. Reinstalling *LeaseWriter*

If *LeaseWriter* becomes unusable because of an unexpected crash or power failure, you will need to reinstall the program from the CD, following the installation instructions in Chapter 2.

> ⚠ **Reinstall to the same folder/location as the damaged files.** *You will not be able to restore data from your backup files unless you reinstall* LeaseWriter *to the exact same folder/location that you originally installed to.*

After you reinstall, you can restore data from your backup files, as described below.

3. Importing Data From Backups

After you have reinstalled, you can restore data that you entered before *LeaseWriter* became damaged. Here's how:

1. Start *LeaseWriter*.
2. Open the Scripts menu.

3. Choose Recover from Backup. This will open a dialog box asking if you want to restore data from the last backup.

4. Click **Restore**.

This process will take a few seconds. When you're done, just resume using *LeaseWriter* as you normally would.

The program should run fine, but you may have lost the data most recently entered prior to the crash. Return to the part of *LeaseWriter* that you were last using; if necessary, re-enter any data that were lost.

F. Contacting Nolo Press Technical Support

If you have problems that are not cleared up in this Troubleshooting chapter, your first step should be to visit the Technical Support page of Nolo Press's Website at:

> http://www.nolo.com/software/TechSupp.html

If you don't find your answer there, contact our Tech Support staff directly:

E-mail	NoloTec@nolo.com
Phone	510-549-4660 between 9:00 A.M. and 5:00 P.M.
	Pacific Time, Monday through Friday. When you call, try to be in front of the computer with which you are having the problem.

Please remember that Tech Support can only help registered users with problems running the *LeaseWriter* program, and cannot provide legal advice concerning drafting *LeaseWriter* documents.

And please have the following information ready (if you phone) or included in your e-mail:

- the version of *LeaseWriter* (should be 1.0 or higher)
- the point in the program where the problem occurred
- whether you can duplicate the problem
- the brand and model of computer you are using
- the brand and model of printer (if you are having trouble printing)
- the operating system and the version you are running (for example, Windows 95 version 4.00, or Macintosh System 7.5.3)
- amount of RAM, and
- if you're using a Mac, any Extensions or Control Panel devices you are running.

To get most of this information about your system:

- In Windows: (1) right-click on the My Computer icon on your desktop; (2) select Properties; and (3) click on the tab that contains the information you need.
- In Macintosh: (1) go to the Finder; and (2) choose About This Macintosh from the Apple menu. ■

Appendix
List of Forms in *LeaseWriter*

This list briefly describes the purpose of each *LeaseWriter* form and where it's located in:

- the *LeaseWriter* program
- this *Users' Guide*, and
- the book *Leases & Rental Agreements*.

For details on when and why to use a particular form, see also its appropriate Help Topics.

CONSENT TO BACKGROUND & REFERENCE CHECK

Purpose: Use this form to get authorization to verify the information and references provided on a tenant's rental application and to run a credit report.

Locations:

LeaseWriter	Forms & Letters - Screening Tenants
Users' Guide	Chapter 7, Section C
Leases & Rental Agreements	Chapter 3

FLORIDA LEASE ADDENDUM

Purpose: This addendum, concerning the return of security deposits, must be completed and added to all Florida leases and rental agreements.

Locations:

LeaseWriter	Create or Change Lease - Lease Interview - Display & Print
	Create or Change Lease - QuickCreate - Preview/Print
	Forms & Letters - Blank Lease Forms
Users' Guide	Chapter 6, Section H
Leases & Rental Agreements	N/A

LANDLORD-TENANT CHECKLIST

Purpose: Use this form to document the condition and furnishings of rental property at move-in time, including a comprehensive list of existing damage and obvious wear and tear. Use this same form at move-out time when you inspect the unit again.

Locations:

LeaseWriter   Forms & Letters - Moving In

Users' Guide   Chapter 7, Section D

Leases & Rental Agreements   Chapter 4

LEAD PAINT HAZARD DISCLOSURE FORM

Purpose: Give this form to tenants to comply with federal lead disclosure laws.

Locations:

LeaseWriter   Create or Change Lease - Lease Interview - Display & Print
Create or Change Lease - QuickCreate - Preview/Print
Forms & Letters - Blank Lease Forms

Users' Guide   Chapter 6, Section H

Leases & Rental Agreements   Chapter 2

LEASE (FIXED TERM)

Purpose: Use this form to draft a lease for a fixed term (such as one year).

Locations:

LeaseWriter   Create or Change Lease - Lease Interview
Create or Change Lease - QuickCreate
Forms & Letters - Blank Lease Forms

Users' Guide   Chapter 6, Sections B-E

Leases & Rental Agreements   Chapter 2

MOVE-OUT LETTER

Purpose: Use this letter to inform tenants what they are expected to do—for example, in terms of cleaning—before vacating the premises at the end of their tenancy.

Locations:

LeaseWriter	Forms & Letters - Moving Out
Users' Guide	Chapter 7, Section F
Leases & Rental Agreements	Chapter 5

NOTICE OF INTENT TO ENTER DWELLING UNIT

Purpose: Use this form to notify the tenant of your intent to enter the rental property.

Locations:

LeaseWriter	Forms & Letters - Repairs, Access & More
Users' Guide	Chapter 7, Section E
Leases & Rental Agreements	Chapter 4

RENTAL AGREEMENT

Purpose: Use this form to draft a month-to-month rental agreement that can be terminated by giving notice (commonly 30 days).

Locations:

LeaseWriter	Create or Change Lease - Lease Interview Create or Change Lease - QuickCreate Forms & Letters - Blank Lease Forms
Users' Guide	Chapter 6, Sections B-E
Leases & Rental Agreements	Chapter 2

RENTAL APPLICATION

Purpose: Use this form to get important information on a prospective tenant's employment, income and credit, past evictions or bankruptcies and references.

Locations:

LeaseWriter	Forms & Letters - Screening Tenants
Users' Guide	Chapter 7, Section C
Leases & Rental Agreements	Chapter 3

RESIDENT'S MAINTENANCE/REPAIR REQUEST

Purpose: Give this form to tenants, so they can make requests for maintenance and repairs.

Locations:

LeaseWriter	Forms & Letters - Repairs, Access and More
Users' Guide	Chapter 7, Section E
Leases & Rental Agreements	Chapter 4

SECURITY DEPOSIT ITEMIZATION

Purpose: Use this form if you are deducting part of the security deposit for repairs, cleaning or unpaid rent.

Locations:

LeaseWriter	Forms & Letters - Moving Out
Users' Guide	Chapter 7, Section F
Leases & Rental Agreements	Chapter 5

SECURITY DEPOSIT: RETURN ENTIRE DEPOSIT

Purpose: Use this form if the entire security deposit is being returned to the tenant.

Locations:

LeaseWriter	Forms & Letters - Moving Out
Users' Guide	Chapter 7, Section F
Leases & Rental Agreements	Chapter 5

TENANT REFERENCES FORM

Purpose: Use this form to screen tenants to fill a vacancy. You can jot down information given by previous landlords, current employers and personal references.

Locations:

LeaseWriter	Forms & Letters - Screening Tenants
Users' Guide	Chapter 7, Section C
Leases & Rental Agreements	Chapter 3

TENANT'S NOTICE OF INTENT TO MOVE OUT

Purpose: Give this form to the tenant to fill out to terminate a month-to-month tenancy.

Locations:

LeaseWriter	Forms & Letters - Moving Out
Users' Guide	Chapter 7, Section F
Leases & Rental Agreements	Chapter 5

TIME ESTIMATE FOR REPAIR

Purpose: Give this form to the tenant explaining when you will make requested repairs to the rental property.

Locations:

LeaseWriter	Forms & Letters - Repairs, Access & More
Users' Guide	Chapter 7, Section E
Leases & Rental Agreements	Chapter 4 ■

LEASEWRITER™

a special LEASEWRITER™ edition of

Leases & Rental Agreements

by Marcia Stewart and Attorneys Janet Portman and Ralph Warner

Table of Contents

4 Getting the Tenant Moved In

5 Changing or Ending a Tenancy

6 How to Find Your State Statutes Online

Index

1

Being a Successful Landlord

The rental agreement or lease that you and your tenant sign is the contractual basis of your relationship. Taken together with the landlord-tenant laws of your state—and, in a few areas, local and federal laws—it sets out almost all the legal rules you and your tenant must follow. Your rental agreement or lease is also an immensely practical document, full of crucial business details, such as how long the tenant can occupy your property and the amount of the rent.

Given their importance, there's no question that you need to create effective and legal rental agreements or leases with your tenants. This book shows you how, by providing clearly written, fair and effective tear-out lease and rental agreement forms, along with clear explanations of each clause.

Our agreements are legally accurate and up-to-date, based on careful research of every state's landlord-tenant laws. They can be tailored to fit the details of your situation. Throughout the book, we suggest ways to do this and also caution you about the types of modifications likely to get you into legal hot water.

In addition to showing you how to prepare a lease or rental agreement, this book also covers key legal issues that landlords need to understand, including how to legally choose tenants and start a tenancy. It also highlights the legal and practical issues involved with changing or ending a tenancy. This book provides forms that supplement a lease and a rental agreement, including a rental application designed to help you choose the best tenant. Other forms, such as a Landlord/Tenant Checklist (used to document the condition of the rental unit at the beginning and end of the tenancy), will help you avoid legal problems with tenants, such as disputes over security deposits.

 Who shouldn't use our lease or rental agreement?

Don't use the forms in this book if you're renting out property that is subsidized by the government, such as the Section 8 program of the federal Department of Housing and Urban Development. You may need to use a special government-drafted lease. Also, our forms should not be used for renting out mobile homes, condominiums, hotels or commercial property.

Ten Tips for Being a Successful Landlord

1. **Don't rent to anyone before checking his credit history, references and background.** Haphazard screening too often results in problems—a tenant who pays the rent late or not at all, trashes your place or moves in undesirable friends—or worse.

2. **Get all the important terms of the tenancy in writing.** Beginning with the rental application and lease or rental agreement, be sure to document important facts of your relationship with your tenants—including when and how you handle tenant complaints and repair problems, notice you must give to enter a tenant's apartment and the like.

3. **Establish a clear, fair system of setting, collecting, holding and returning security deposits.** Inspect and document the condition of the rental unit before the tenant moves in to avoid disputes over security deposits when the tenant moves out.

4. **Stay on top of repair and maintenance needs and make repairs when requested.** If the property is not kept in good repair, you'll alienate good tenants. And they may have the right to withhold rent, sue for any injuries caused by defective conditions, or move out without notice.

5. **Don't let your tenants and property be easy marks for a criminal.** You could well be liable for the tenant's losses. Landlords are sued more than any other group of business owners in the country. The average settlement paid by a landlord's insurance company is $600,000, and the average jury award is $1.2 million.

6. **Respect your tenants' privacy.** Notify tenants whenever you plan to enter their rental unit, and provide as much notice as possible, at least 24 hours or the minimum amount required by state law.

7. **Disclose environmental hazards such as lead.** Landlords are increasingly being held liable for tenant health problems resulting from exposure to environmental poisons in the rental premises.

8. **Choose and supervise your manager carefully.** If a manager commits a crime or is incompetent, you may be held financially responsible. Do a thorough background check and clearly spell out the manager's duties, to help prevent problems down the road.

9. **Purchase enough liability and other property insurance.** A well-designed insurance program can protect your rental property from losses caused by everything from fire and storms to burglary, vandalism and personal injury and discrimination lawsuits.

10. **Try to resolve disputes with tenants without lawyers and lawsuits.** If you have a conflict with a tenant over rent, repairs, your access to the rental unit, noise or some other issue that doesn't immediately warrant an eviction, meet with the tenant to see if the problem can be resolved informally. If that doesn't work, consider mediation by a neutral third party, often available at little or no cost from a publicly funded program. If your dispute involves money and all attempts to reach agreement fail, try small claims court, where you can represent yourself. Use it to collect unpaid rent or to seek money for property damage after a tenant moves out and the deposit is exhausted.

Icons Used in This Book

Related Topics
This icon lets you know where you can read more about the particular issue or topic discussed in the text.

Warning
Slow down and consider potential problems.

Fast Track
You may be able to skip some material that doesn't apply to your situation.

Form in LeaseWriter
LeaseWriter includes the form discussed in the text.

Tip
A practical tip or good idea.

Rent Control
A rent control ordinance may address the issue discussed in the text.

Briefcase
You probably need the advice of a lawyer who specializes in landlord-tenant law.

Every Landlord's Legal Guide

A lease or rental agreement is only one part of a landlord-tenant legal relationship. For example, many state (and some federal and local) laws are also extremely important. A comprehensive explanation of these laws, and the practical steps rental property owners can take to comply with them (while at the same time running an efficient and profitable business), is covered in *Every Landlord's Legal Guide*, by Marcia Stewart, Ralph Warner and Janet Portman (Nolo Press).

Every Landlord's Legal Guide covers most key laws affecting landlords in all 50 states, including your repair and maintenance responsibilities and your liability for crime and environmental hazards such as lead. *Every Landlord's Legal Guide* covers rules and procedures for collecting and returning security deposits, anti-discrimination laws, privacy rules, employment laws affecting managers, how to resolve problems with tenants or begin the eviction process and more. It includes over 20 legal forms on disk and in tear-out form.

Get a Little Help From Your Friends

Many landlords have discovered the value of belonging to a local or state association of rental property owners. These organizations range from small, volunteer-run groups to substantial city, county or even statewide organizations with paid staff and lobbyists. Many offer a wide variety of support and services to their members, including the following:

- legal information and updates through newsletters, publications, seminars and other means
- tenant screening and credit check services
- training and practical advice on compliance with legal responsibilities
- a place to meet other rental property owners and exchange information and ideas, and
- referrals to knowledgeable and appropriately priced professionals, including attorneys, accountants, maintenance firms and property management companies.

If you can't find an association of rental property owners in your phone book, ask other landlords for references. You can also contact the National Apartment Association (NAA), a national organization whose members include many individual state associations:

National Apartment Association
201 North Union Street, Suite 200
Alexandria, Virginia 22314
703-518-6141

The National Multi-Housing Council, a national organization of many of the country's largest landlords, may also be helpful:

National Multi-Housing Council
1850 M Street, Suite 540, NW
Washington, DC 20036
202-659-3381

2

Preparing a Lease or Rental Agreement

This chapter provides step-by-step instructions on how to prepare a lease or rental agreement form. It discusses important issues that relate to your choices—as to both the type of document and the specific provisions—including any state, federal and local laws that may apply.

 The lease and rental agreement forms are legally sound as designed. *If you change important terms or make major changes, however, you may affect a form's legal validity. In this case, you may wish to have your work reviewed by an experienced landlords' lawyer.*

A. Which Is Better, a Lease or a Rental Agreement?

One of the key decisions you need to make is whether to use a lease or a rental agreement. Often, but by no means always, your choice will depend on how long you want a tenant to stay. But, since other factors can also come into play, read what follows carefully before evaluating your own situation and making a decision.

1. Month-to-Month Rental Agreement

A written rental agreement provides for a tenancy for a short period of time. The law refers to these agreements as periodic or month-to-month tenancies, although it is often legally possible to base them on other time periods, as would be the case if the rent must be paid every two weeks. A month-to-month tenancy automatically renews each month—or other agreed-upon period—unless the landlord or tenant gives the other the proper amount of written notice (typically 30 days) and terminates the agreement.

Month-to-month rental agreements give you more flexibility than leases. You may increase the rent or change other terms of the tenancy on relatively short notice (subject to any restrictions of local rent control ordinances— see Clause 5, below). And with proper notice, you may also end the tenancy at any time (again, subject to any rent control restrictions). (Chapter 5 discusses notice requirements to change or end a rental agreement.) Not surprisingly, many landlords prefer to rent month-to-month, particularly in urban areas with tight rental markets where new tenants are usually easily found and rents are trending upwards.

On the flip side, a month-to-month tenancy almost guarantees more tenant turnover. Tenants who may legally move out with only 30 days' notice may be more inclined to do so than tenants who make a longer commitment. Some landlords base their rental business strategy on painstakingly seeking high-quality, long-term renters. If you're one of those, or if you live in an area where it's difficult to fill vacancies, you will probably want tenants to commit for a longer period, such as a year. As discussed below, a fixed-term lease, especially when combined with tenant-friendly management policies, may encourage tenants to stay longer. However, it is no guarantee against turnover.

2. Fixed-Term Lease

A lease is a contract that obligates both you and the tenant for a set period of time—usually six months or a year, but sometimes longer. With a fixed-term lease, you can't raise the rent or change other terms of the tenancy until the lease runs out, unless the lease itself allows future changes or the tenant agrees in writing to the changes.

In addition, you usually can neither ask a tenant to move out nor can prevail in an eviction lawsuit before the lease term expires unless the tenant fails to pay the rent or violates another significant term of the lease or state law, such as repeatedly making too much noise, damaging the rental unit or selling drugs on your property. This restriction can sometimes be problematic if you end up with a tenant you would like to be rid of but don't have sufficient cause to evict.

To take but one example, if you wish to sell the property halfway into the lease, the existence of long-term tenants—especially if they are paying less than the market rate—may be a negative factor. The new owner usually purchases all the obligations of the previous owner, including the obligation to honor existing leases. Of course, the opposite can also be true—if you have good, long-term tenants paying a fair rent, the property may be very attractive to potential new owners.

At the end of the lease term, you have several options. You can:

- decline to renew the lease, except in the few areas where local rent control requirements prohibit it

- sign a new lease for a set period, or
- do nothing—which means, under the law of most states, your lease will usually turn into a month-to-month tenancy if you continue to accept monthly rent from the tenant.

(Chapter 5 discusses in more detail how fixed-term leases end.)

Although leases restrict your flexibility, there's often a big plus to having long-term tenants. Some tenants make a serious personal commitment when they enter into a long-term lease, in part because they think they'll be liable for several months' rent if they leave early. And people who plan to be with you over the long term are often more likely to respect your property and the rights of other tenants, making the management of your rental units far easier and more pleasant.

 A lease guarantees less income security than you think.

As experienced landlords know well, it's usually not hard for a determined tenant to break a lease and avoid paying all of the money theoretically owed for the unused portion of the lease term. A few states allow tenants to break a lease without penalty in specific circumstances, such as a change in employment. And many states require landlords to "mitigate" (minimize) the loss they suffer as a result of a broken lease—meaning that if a tenant moves out early, you must try to find another suitable tenant at the same or a greater rent. If you re-rent the unit immediately (or if a judge believes it could have been re-rented with a reasonable effort), the lease-breaking tenant is off the hook—except, perhaps, for a small obligation to

pay for the few days or weeks the unit was vacant plus any costs you incurred in re-renting it. (Chapter 5, Section C, discusses a landlord's responsibility to mitigate damages if the tenant leaves early.)

As mentioned, you'll probably prefer to use leases in areas where there is a high vacancy rate or it is difficult to find tenants for one season of the year. For example, if you are renting near a college that is in session for only nine months a year, or in a vacation area that is deserted for months, you are far better off with a year's lease. This is especially true if you have the market clout to charge a large deposit, so that a tenant who wants to leave early has an incentive to find someone to take over the tenancy.

 Always put your agreement in writing.

Oral leases or rental agreements are perfectly legal for month-to-month tenancies and for leases of a year or less in most states. While oral agreements are easy and informal, it is never wise to use one. As time passes, people's memories (even yours) have a funny habit of becoming unreliable. You can almost count on tenants claiming that you made, but didn't keep, certain oral promises—for example, to repaint their kitchen or not to increase the rent. Tenants may also forget their own key agreements, such as no subletting. And other issues—for example, how deposits may be used—probably aren't covered at all. Oral leases are especially dangerous because they require that both

parties accurately remember one important term—the length of the lease—over a considerable time. If something goes wrong with an oral rental agreement or lease, you and your tenants are all too likely to end up in court, arguing over who said what to whom, when and in what context.

B. Completing the Lease or Rental Agreement Form

This section explains each clause in the lease and rental agreement forms that are provided in this book. Both forms cover the basic terms of the tenancy (such as the amount of rent and date due). Except for Clause 4, Term of the Tenancy, the lease and rental agreement forms are identical.

Read the detailed instructions carefully. If there is one area of landlord-tenant law where details count, this is it. Make sure you really do have the information necessary to create a lease or a rental agreement that accurately reflects your business strategy and complies with all the laws of your state.

LeaseWriter includes Month-to-Month Rental Agreement and Fixed-Term Residential Lease forms. A filled-in sample rental agreement is shown at the end of this chapter.

Clause 1. Identification of Landlord and Tenant

This Agreement is entered into between
_____ ("Tenant")
and _____
("Landlord"). Each Tenant is jointly and severally liable for the payment of rent and performance of all other terms of this Agreement.

Every lease or rental agreement must identify the tenant and the landlord or the property owner—usually called the "parties" to the agreement. The term "Agreement" (a synonym for contract) refers to either the lease or rental agreement.

Any competent adult—at least 18 years of age—may be a party to a lease or rental agreement. (A teenager under age 18 may also be a party to a lease if he or she has achieved legal adult status through a court order, military service or marriage.)

The last sentence of Clause 1 states that if you have more than one tenant, they (the cotenants) are all "jointly and severally" liable for paying rent and abiding by all the terms of the agreement. This essential bit of legalese simply means that each tenant is legally responsible for the whole rent and complying with the lease. This part of the clause gives you important rights; it means you can legally seek the entire rent from any one of the tenants should the others skip out or be unable to pay. A "jointly and severally liable" clause also gives you the right to evict all of the tenants even if just one has broken the terms of the lease—for example, by seriously damaging the property, or moving in an extra roommate or a dog, contrary to the lease or a rental agreement.

How to Fill In Clause 1:

Fill in the names of all tenants—adults who will live in the premises, including both members of a married couple. It's crucial that everyone who lives in your rental unit signs the lease or the rental agreement. This underscores your expectation that each individual is responsible for the rent and the use of the property. Also, make sure the tenant's name matches his or her legal documents, such as a driver's license. You may set a reasonable limit on the number of people per rental unit. (See "How Many Tenants to Allow," below.)

In the last blank, list the names of all landlords or property owners.

 Chapter 3 provides detailed advice on choosing tenants.

Clause 2. Identification of Premises

Subject to the terms and conditions in this Agreement, Landlord rents to Tenant, and Tenant rents from Landlord, for residential purposes only, the premises located at _____
("the premises"), together with the following furnishings and appliances:

_____
_____ .

Rental of the premises also includes
_____
_____ .

Clause 2 identifies the location of the property being rented (the premises) and provides details on furnishings. The words "for residential purposes only" are to prevent a tenant from using the property for conducting a business that might affect your insurance or violate zoning laws.

How to Fill In Clause 2:

Fill in the address of the unit or house you are renting. If there is an apartment or building number, specify that as well as the city and state.

Add as much detail as necessary to clarify what's included in—or excluded from—the rental premises, such as a kitchen table. If the rental unit is fully furnished, state that here and provide detailed information on the Landlord/Tenant Checklist included in Chapter 4.

In some circumstances, you may want to elaborate on exactly what the premises include. For example, if the rental unit includes a parking space, storage in the garage or basement, or other use of the property, such as a gardening shed in the backyard or the use of a barn in rural areas, specifically include it in your description of the premises.

Possible Modifications to Clause 2:

If a particular part of the rental property that a tenant might reasonably assume to be included is not being rented, such as a garage or storage shed you wish to use yourself or rent to someone else, explicitly exclude it from your description of the premises.

 Investigate before letting a tenant run a business on the premises.

Over 20 million Americans run a business from their house or apartment. If a tenant asks you to modify Clause 2 to allow him to operate a business, you have some checking to do—even if you are disposed to say yes. For starters, you'll need to check local zoning laws for restrictions on home-based businesses, including the type of businesses allowed (if any), the amount of car and truck traffic the business can generate, outside signs, on-street parking, the number of employees, and the percentage of floor space devoted to the business. You'll also want to consult your insurance company as to whether you'll need a more expensive policy to cover the potential liability of employees or guests. In many places, a home office for occasional use will not be a problem. But if the tenant wants to operate a business that involves people and deliveries coming and going, such as a therapy practice, jewelry importer or small business consulting firm, you should seriously consider whether neighboring tenants will be inconvenienced. (Where will visitors park, for example?) You may also want to require that the tenant maintain certain types of liability insurance, so that you won't wind up paying if someone gets hurt on the rental property—for example, a business customer who trips and falls on the front steps. Also, be aware that if you allow a residence to be used as a commercial site, your property may need to meet the accessibility requirements of the federal Americans With Disabilities Act (commonly known as the ADA). For more information on the ADA, contact the Department of Justice, Office on the Americans With Disabilities Act, Civil Rights Division, in Washington, D.C., at 202-514-0301.

Clause 3. Limits on Use and Occupancy

The premises are to be used only as a private residence for Tenant(s) listed in Clause 1 of this Agreement, and their minor children. Occupancy by guests for more than _____ is prohibited without Landlord's written consent and will be considered a breach of this Agreement.

Clause 3 specifies that the rental unit is only the residence of the tenants and their minor children. It lets the tenants know that they may not move anyone else in as a permanent resident without your consent. The value of this clause is that a tenant who tries to move in a relative or friend for a longer period has clearly violated a defined standard, which gives you grounds for eviction.

Clause 3 also includes a time limit for guest stays. Even if you do not plan to strictly enforce restrictions on guests, this provision will be very handy if a tenant tries to move in a friend or relative for a month or two, calling her a guest. It will give you the leverage you need to ask the guest to leave, request that the guest become a tenant with an appropriate increase in rent or, if necessary, evict the tenant for violating this lease provision.

How to Fill In Clause 3:

Fill in the number of days you allow guests to stay without your consent. We suggest you allow up to ten days in any six-month period, but of course you may want to modify this based on your own experience.

 Don't discriminate against families with children.

You can legally establish reasonable space-to-people ratios, but you cannot use overcrowding as an excuse for refusing to rent to tenants with children, especially if you would rent to the same number of adults. (See "How Many Tenants to Allow," below.) Discrimination against families with children is illegal, except in housing reserved for senior citizens only. Just as important as adopting a reasonable people-to-square-foot standard in the first place is the maintenance of a consistent occupancy policy. If you allow three adults to live in a two-bedroom apartment, you had better let a couple with a child live in the same type of unit, or you are leaving yourself open to charges that you are illegally discriminating.

Clause 4. Term of the Tenancy

This clause sets out the key difference between a lease and a rental agreement: how long a rent-paying tenant is entitled to stay.

Section A, above, discusses the pros and cons of leases and rental agreements, including notice requirements to change or end a tenancy.

a. Lease Provision

The term of the rental will begin on _____, 199___, and end on _____, 199___. If Tenant vacates before the term ends, Tenant will be liable for the balance of the rent for the remainder of the term.

This lease provision sets a definite date for the beginning and the expiration of the lease and obligates both the landlord and the tenant for a specific term.

Most leases run for one year. This makes sense because it allows you to raise the rent at reasonably frequent intervals if market conditions allow. Leases may be shorter (six months) or longer (24 months). This, of course, is up to you and the tenants. A long period—two, three or even five years—can be appropriate, for example, if you're renting out your own house because you're taking a two-year sabbatical or if you have agreed to allow a tenant to make major repairs or remodel your property at his expense.

How to Fill In Clause 4 (Lease):

In the blanks, fill in the starting date and the expiration date of the lease.

b. Rental Agreement Provision

The rental will begin on
_____, 199__, and continue on a month-to-month basis. Landlord may terminate the tenancy or modify the terms of this Agreement by giving the Tenant ____ days' written notice. Tenant may terminate the tenancy by giving the Landlord ____ days' written notice.

This rental agreement provides for a month-to-month tenancy and specifies how much written notice you must give a tenant to change or end a tenancy, and how much notice the tenant must provide you before moving

out. (See Chapter 5, Section B, for a sample Tenant's Notice of Intent to Move Out form.)

How to Fill In Clause 4 (Rental Agreement):

In the first blank, fill in the date the tenancy will begin.

In the next two blanks, fill in the amount of written notice you'll need to give tenants to end or change a tenancy and the amount of notice tenants must provide to end a tenancy. In most cases, to comply with the law of your state, this will be 30 days for both landlord and tenant in a month-to-month tenancy. (See the the 50-State Law Browser for a list of your state's notice requirements.)

Possible Modifications to Clause 4 (Rental Agreement):

This rental agreement is month-to-month, although you can change it to a different interval as long as you don't go below the minimum notice period required by your state's law. If you do, be aware that notice requirements to change or end a tenancy may also need to differ from those required for standard month-to-month rental agreements, since state law often requires that all key notice periods be the same.

Your right to terminate or change the terms of a tenancy, even one from month-to-month, can be limited by a rent control ordinance. Check local rules for details.

How Many Tenants to Allow

Two kinds of laws affect the number of people who may live in a rental unit.

State and local health and safety codes typically set *maximum* limits on the number of tenants, based on the size of the unit and the number of bedrooms and bathrooms.

Even more important, the federal government has taken the lead in establishing *minimum* limits on the number of tenants, through passage of the Fair Housing Act (42 U.S. Code §§ 3601-3619, 3631) and by means of regulations from the Department of Housing and Urban Development (HUD). HUD generally considers a limit of two persons per bedroom a reasonable occupancy standard. Because the number of bedrooms is not the only factor—the size of the bedrooms and configuration of the rental unit are also considered—the federal test has become known as the "two per bedroom plus" standard. States and localities can set their own occupancy standards as long as they are more generous than the federal government's—that is, by allowing more people per rental unit.

The Fair Housing Act is designed primarily to disallow illegal discrimination against families with children, but it also allows you to establish your own "reasonable" restrictions on the number of people per rental unit—as long as your policy is truly tied to health and safety needs. In addition, you can adopt standards that are driven by a legitimate business reason or necessity, such as the capacities of the plumbing or electrical systems. Your personal preferences (such as a desire to reduce wear and tear by limiting the number of occupants or to ensure a quiet, uncrowded environment for upscale tenants), however, do not constitute a legitimate business reason. If your occupancy policy limits the number of tenants for any reason other than health, safety and legitimate business needs, you risk charges that you are discriminating against families.

Figuring out whether your occupancy policy is legal is not always a simple matter. Furthermore, laws on occupancy limits often change. For more information, call HUD's Fair Housing Information Clearinghouse at 800-343-3442. Check your local and state housing authority for other occupancy standards that may affect your rental property.

The 50-State Law Browser includes state fair housing agencies.

Clause 5. Payment of Rent

Regular monthly rent.

Tenant will pay to Landlord a monthly rent of $_____, payable in advance on the first day of each month, except when that day falls on a weekend or legal holiday, in which case rent is due on the next business day. Rent will be paid in the following manner, unless Landlord designates otherwise:

Delivery of payment.

Rent will be paid:

☐ by mail, to _____

☐ in person, at _____

Form of payment.

Landlord will accept payment in these forms:

☐ personal check made payable to

_____

☐ cashier's check made payable to

_____

☐ credit card

☐ money order

☐ cash

Prorated first month's rent.

For the period from Tenant's move-in date, _____, 199__, through the end of the month, Tenant will pay to Landlord the prorated monthly rent of $_____. This amount will be paid on or before the date the Tenant moves in.

This clause provides details on the amount of rent and when, where and how it's paid. It requires the tenant to pay rent monthly on the first day of the month, unless the first day falls on a weekend or a legal holiday, in which case rent is due on the next business day. (Extend-

ing the rent due date for holidays is legally required in some states and is a general rule in most.)

How to Fill In Clause 5:

Regular monthly rent. In the first blank, state the amount of monthly rent. Unless your premises are subject to a local rent control ordinance, you can legally charge as much rent as you want (or, more practically speaking, as much as a tenant will pay).

Delivery of payment. Next, specify to whom and where the rent is to be paid—by mail (most common) or in person (if so, specify the address, such as your office or to your manager at the rental unit).

Form of payment. Note all the forms of payment you'll accept, such as personal check and money order.

 Don't accept cash unless you have no choice.

You face an increased risk of robbery if word gets out that you are taking in large amounts of cash once or twice a month. And if you accept cash knowing that the tenant earned it from an illegal act, such as drug dealing, the government could seize the money from you under federal and state forfeiture laws. For both these reasons, we recommend that you insist that rent be paid by check, money order or credit card. If you do accept cash, be sure to provide a written, dated receipt stating the tenant's name and the amount of rent paid. Such a receipt is required by law in a few states, and it's a good idea everywhere.

Prorated first month's rent. If the tenant moves in before the regular rental period—let's say in the middle of the month, and you want rent due on the first of every month—you can specify the prorated amount due for the first partial month. To figure out prorated rent, divide the monthly rent by 30 days and multiply by the number of days in the first rental period. That will avoid confusion about what you expect to be paid. Enter the move-in date, such as "June 21, 199X," and the amount of prorated monthly rent.

EXAMPLE: Meg rents an apartment for $900 per month, with rent due on the first of the month. She moves in on June 21, so she should pay ten days' prorated rent of $300 when she moves in. ($900/30=$30X10 days=$300.) The full $900 July rent is due on July 1.

If the tenant is moving in on the first of the month, or the same day rent is due, write in "N/A" or "Not Applicable" in the section on prorated rent.

Possible Modifications to Clause 5:

Here are a few common ways to modify Clause 5:
Rent due date. You can establish a rent due date different from the first of the month, such as the day of the month on which the tenant moves in. For example, if the tenant moved in on July 10, rent would be due on that date, a system which of course saves the trouble of prorating the first month's rent.

Frequency of rent payments. **You are not** legally required to have your tenant pay rent on a monthly basis. You can modify the clause and require that the rent be paid twice a month, each week or by whatever schedule suits you.

Rent Control

Communities in only five states—California, the District of Columbia, Maryland, New Jersey and New York—have laws that limit the amount of rent landlords may charge and how and when rent may be increased. Typically, only a few cities or counties in each of these states have enacted local rent control ordinances (also called rent stabilization, maximum rent regulation or a similar term), but often these are some of the state's largest cities—for example, San Francisco, Los Angeles, New York City and Newark all have some form of rent control.

Rent control laws commonly regulate much more than rent. For example, owners of rent-controlled properties must often follow specific "just cause" eviction procedures. And local rent control ordinances may require that your lease or rental agreement include certain information—for example, the address of the local rent control board.

If you own rental property in a city that has rent control, you should always have a current copy of the ordinance and any regulations interpreting it. Check with your local rent control board or city manager's or mayor's office for more information on rent control and modify your forms accordingly.

- *Collecting deposits and potential problems with calling a deposit the "last month's rent": Clause 8, this chapter*
- *The value of highlighting your rent rules in a move-in letter to new tenants and collecting the first month's rent: Chapter 4*
- *Tenant's obligations to pay rent when breaking a lease: Chapter 5*
- *Legal citations for state rent rules: 50-state Law Browser.*

Clause 6. Late Charges

If Tenant fails to pay the rent in full before the end of the _____ day after it's due, Tenant will pay Landlord a late charge as follows:

_____

_____ .

Landlord does not waive the right to insist on payment of the rent in full on the date it is due.

It is your legal right to charge a late fee if rent is not paid on time. This clause spells out details of your policy on late fees. A few states have statutes that put precise limits on the amount of late fees or when they can be collected. (The 50-State Law Browser provides details on state laws restricting late rent fees.)

Some rent control ordinances also regulate late fees. If you own rental units in a municipality with rent control, check the ordinances carefully.

But even if your state doesn't have specific rules restricting late fees, you are still bound by general legal principles (often expressed in court decisions) that prohibit unreasonably high fees. Unless your state imposes more specific statutory rules on late fees, you should be on safe ground if you adhere to these principles:

- The total late charge should not exceed 4%-5% of the rent.
- If the late fee increases each day the rent is late, it should be moderate and have an upper limit. A late charge that increases without a maximum could be considered interest charged at an illegal ("usurious") rate. Although state usury laws don't directly apply to late charges, judges often use these laws as one guideline in judging whether a particular provision is reasonable. Most states set their maximum interest rate at about 10% to 12%. A late charge that would generally be acceptable would be a charge of $10 if rent is not paid by the end of the second business day after it is due, plus $5 for each additional day, up to a maximum of 5% of the monthly rental amount.

Don't try to disguise excessive late charges by giving a "discount" for early payment.

One landlord we know concluded that he couldn't get away with charging a $50 late charge on a $425 rent payment, so instead, he designed a rental agreement calling for a rent of $475 with a $50 discount if the rent was not more than three days late. Ingenious as this ploy sounds, it is unlikely to stand up in court in many states unless the discount for timely payment is modest. Giving a relatively large discount is in effect the same as charging an excessive late fee, and a judge is likely to see it as such.

How to Fill In Clause 6:

In the first blank, specify if you will allow a grace period before you charge a late fee. You don't have to give a grace period, but many landlords don't charge a late fee until the rent is two or three days late. If you don't allow any grace period, simply cross out the first blank and the word "after," so that the first line reads "If Tenant fails to pay the rent in full before the end of the day it's due...."

Next, fill in details on your late rent fee, such as the daily charge and any maximum fee.

Possible Modifications to Clause 6:

If you decide not to charge a late fee (something we consider highly unwise), you may simply delete this clause, or write the words "N/A" or "Not Applicable" on it.

Clause 7. Returned Check and Other Bank Charges

If any check offered by Tenant to Landlord in payment of rent or any other amount due under this Agreement is returned for lack of sufficient funds, a "stop payment" or any other reason, Tenant will pay Landlord a returned check charge of $_____.

As with late charges, any bounced-check charges you require must be reasonable. Generally, you should charge no more than the amount your bank charges you for a returned check, probably $10 to $20 per returned item, plus a few dollars for your trouble.

 Don't tolerate repeated bad checks.

If a tenant habitually pays rent late or gives you bad checks, give written notice demanding that the tenant pay the rent or move within a few days. How long the tenant is allowed to stay depends on state law; in most places, it's about three to 15 days. In most instances, the tenant who receives this kind of "pay rent or quit" notice pays up, reforms his ways and that's the end of it. But if the tenant doesn't pay the rent (or move), you can file an eviction lawsuit. An alternative is to serve the tenant with a 30-day notice to change Clause 5 of the lease or rental agreement to require payment with a money order or a verified credit card transaction.

How to Fill In Clause 7:

In the blank, fill in the amount of the returned check charge. If you won't accept checks, fill in "N/A" or "Not Applicable."

Clause 8. Security Deposit

On signing this Agreement, Tenant will pay to Landlord the sum of $_____ as a security deposit. Tenant may not, without Landlord's prior written consent, apply this security deposit to the last month's rent or to any other sum due under this Agreement. Within _____ after Tenant has vacated the premises, returned keys and provided Landlord with a forwarding address, Landlord will return the deposit in full or give Tenant an itemized written statement of the reasons for, and the dollar amount of, any of the security deposit retained by Landlord, along with a check for any deposit balance.

Most landlords quite sensibly ask for a security deposit before entrusting hundreds of thousands of dollars worth of real estate to a tenant. But it's easy to get into legal trouble over deposits, because they are strictly regulated by state law, and sometimes also by city ordinance. The law of most states dictates how large a deposit you can require, how you can use it, when you must return it and more. Several states require you to put deposits in a separate account and pay interest on them.

The use and return of security deposits is a frequent source of disputes between landlords and tenants. To avoid confusion and legal hassles, this clause is clear on the subject, including:

- the dollar amount of the deposit
- the fact that the deposit may not be used for the last month's rent without your prior approval, and
- when the deposit will be returned, along with an itemized statement of deductions.

This section discusses the basic information you need to complete Clause 8. Check the 50-State Law Browser for specific security deposit rules that apply to your situation.

If, after reviewing these tables, you have any questions of what's allowed in your state, you should get a current copy of your state's security deposit statute or an up-to-date summary from a landlords' association. In addition, be sure to check local ordinances in all areas where you own property. Cities, particularly those with rent control, may add additional rules on security deposits, such as a limit on the amount you can charge or a requirement that you pay interest on deposits.

Basic State Rules on Security Deposits

All states allow you to collect a security deposit when a tenant moves in and hold it until the tenant leaves. The general purpose of a security deposit is to assure that a tenant pays the rent when it is due and keeps the rental unit in good condition. Rent you collect in advance for the first month is not typically considered part of the security deposit.

State laws typically control the amount you can charge and how and when you must return security deposits.

- Many states limit the amount you can collect as a deposit to a maximum of one or two months' rent. Sometimes, the limit in a particular state is higher for furnished units.

- Several states require landlords to pay tenants interest on security deposits, and establish detailed requirements as to the interest rate that must be paid. Some states require you to put deposits in a separate account, sometimes called a "trust" account, rather than mixing the funds with your personal or business accounts. In most states, however, you don't have to pay tenants interest on deposits or put them in a separate bank account. In other words, you can simply put the money in your pocket or bank account and use it, as long as you have it available when the tenant moves out.

- When a tenant moves out, you will have a set amount of time (usually from 14 to 30 days, depending on the state) to either return the tenant's entire deposit or provide an itemized statement of deductions and refund any deposit balance.

- You can generally withhold all or part of the deposit to pay for:
  1. Unpaid rent
  2. Repairing damage to the premises (except for "ordinary wear and tear") caused by the tenant, a family member or guest

  3. Cleaning necessary to restore the rental unit to its condition at the beginning of the tenancy (over and above "ordinary wear and tear")
  4. Restoring or replacing rental unit property taken by the tenant. States typically also allow you to use a deposit to cover the tenant's other obligations under the lease or rental agreement, which may include payment of utility charges or parking fees.

- The laws of many states set heavy penalties for violation of security deposit statutes. (See Chapter 5, Section D.)

How Much Deposit Should You Charge?

Normally, the best advice is to charge as much as the market will bear, within any legal limits. The more the tenant has at stake, the better the chance your property will be respected. And the larger the deposit, the more financial protection you will have if a tenant leaves owing you rent.

The market, however, often keeps the practical limit on deposits lower than the maximum allowed by law. Your common sense and your business sense need to work together in setting security deposits. Here are a number of considerations to keep in mind:

- **Charge the full limit in high-risk situations**—where there's a lot of tenant turnover, if the tenant has a pet and

Don't Charge Nonrefundable Deposits

State laws are often muddled on the subject of whether charging nonrefundable deposits and fees is legal. Some specifically allow landlords to collect a fee that is not refundable—such as for pets, cleaning or redecorating—as long as this is clearly stated in the lease or rental agreement. But many states—and this is clearly the trend—have enacted security deposit statutes that specifically prohibit nonrefundable fees, such as a fixed fee for cleaning drapes or carpets or for painting; all such fees are legally considered security deposits, no matter what they are labeled in the lease or rental agreement, and must be refundable. It is also illegal in many states to make the return of deposits contingent upon a tenant staying for a minimum period of time.

Generally, it's best to avoid the legal uncertainties and not try to collect any nonrefundable fees from tenants. In addition, most landlords have found that making all deposits refundable avoids many time-consuming arguments and even lawsuits with tenants. We believe it's much simpler just to consider the expenses these fees cover as part of your overhead and figure them into the rent, raising it, if necessary.

If you have a specific concern about a particular tenant—for example, you're afraid a tenant's pet will damage the carpets or furniture—just ask for a higher security deposit (but do check your state's maximum). That way, you're covered if the pet causes damage, and if it doesn't, the tenant won't have to shell out unnecessarily.

If, despite our advice, you want to charge a nonrefundable fee, check your state's law to find what (if any) kinds of nonrefundable fees are allowed. Then, make sure your lease or rental agreement is clear on the subject.

you're concerned about damage, or if the tenant's credit is shaky and you're worried about unpaid rent.

- **Consider the psychological advantage of a higher rent rather than a high deposit.** Many tenants would rather pay a slightly higher rent than an enormous deposit. Also, many acceptable, solvent tenants have a hard time coming up with several months' rent, especially if they are still in a rental unit and are awaiting the return of a previous security deposit.

- **Charge a bigger deposit for single-family homes.** Unlike multiunit residences, where close-by neighbors or a manager can spot, report and quickly stop any destruction of the premises, the single-family home is somewhat of an island. The condition of the interior and even the exterior may be hard to assess, unless you live close by or can frequently check the condition of a single-family rental. And, of course, the cost of repairing damage to a house is likely to be higher than for an apartment.

- **Gain a marketing advantage by allowing a deposit to be paid in installments.** If rentals are plentiful in your area, with comparable units renting at about the same price, you might gain a competitive edge by allowing tenants to pay the deposit in several installments, rather than one lump sum.
- **Charge less than one month's rent to discourage tenants from considering the deposit as simply the last month's rent.** Somewhat surprisingly, many landlords have found that charging a little less than the last month's rent results in fewer tenants assuming (incorrectly) that the deposit is simply an advance payment for their last month's rent and thus refusing to pay rent the last month.

> **Require renter's insurance as an alternative to a high security deposit.**
> *If you're worried about damage but don't think you can raise the deposit any higher, require renter's insurance. You can give your property an extra measure of protection by insisting that the tenant purchase renter's insurance, which may cover damage done by the tenant or guests. (See the "Renter's Insurance" discussion under Clause 11.)*

Last Month's Rent

It's a common—but often unwise—practice to collect a sum of money called "last month's rent" from a tenant who's moving in. Landlords tend to treat this money as just another security deposit, and use it to cover not only the last month's rent but also other expenses such as repairs or cleaning.

Problems can arise because some states restrict the use of money labeled as the "last month's rent" to its stated purpose: the rent for the tenant's last month of occupancy. If you use any of it to repair damage by the former tenant, you're violating the law. Also, using the "last month's rent" for cleaning and repairs may lead to a dispute with a tenant who feels that the last month's rent is taken care of and resents having to pay all or part of it. You would be better off if the tenant paid the last month's rent when it came due, leaving the entire security deposit available to cover cleaning and repairs.

Avoiding the term "last month's rent" also keeps things simpler if you raise the rent, but not the deposit, before the tenant's last month of occupancy. The problem arises when rent for the tenant's last month becomes due. Has the tenant already paid in full, or does he owe more because the monthly rent is now higher? Legally, there is often no clear answer. In practice, it's a hassle you are best to avoid by not labeling any part of the security deposit "last month's rent."

Clause 8 of the form agreements makes it clear that the tenant may not apply the security deposit to the last month's rent.

How to Fill In Clause 8:

Once you decide how much security deposit you can charge (see the security deposit rules section of the 50-State Law Browser), fill in the amount in the first blank. Unless there's a lower limit, we suggest about two months as your rent deposit, assuming your potential tenants can afford that much. (See "How Much Deposit Should You Charge?" above.) In no case is it wise to charge much less than one month's rent.

Next, fill in the time period when you will return the deposit, using the security deposit rules section of the 50-State Law Browser. If there is no statutory deadline for returning the deposit, we recommend 14 to 21 days as a reasonable time to return a tenant's deposit. Establishing a fairly short period (even if the law of your state allows more time) will discourage anxious tenants from repeatedly bugging you or your manager for their deposit refund. (See the Chapter 5, Section D, discussion of returning security deposits.)

Possible Modifications to Clause 8:

The laws of several states require you to give tenants written information on various aspects of the security deposit, including where the security deposit is being held, interest payments and the terms of and conditions under which the security deposit may be withheld. LeaseWriter provides details on these requirements.

Even if it's not required, you may want to provide additional details on security deposits in your lease or rental agreement. Here are optional clauses you may add to the end of Clause 8.

The security deposit will be held at: _____ (name and address of financial institution).

Landlord will pay Tenant interest on all security deposits as follows: _____(interest terms)_____.

Landlord may withhold only that portion of Tenant's security deposit necessary to: (1) remedy any default by Tenant in the payment of rent; (2) repair damage to the premises, except for ordinary wear and tear caused by Tenant; (3) clean the premises if necessary, and (4) compensate Landlord for any other losses as allowed by state law.

Clause 9. Utilities

Tenant will pay all utility charges, except for the following, which will be paid by Landlord:

_____

_____

This clause helps prevent misunderstandings as to who's responsible for paying utilities. Normally, landlords pay for garbage (and sometimes water, if there is a yard) to help make sure that the premises are well maintained. Tenants usually pay for other services, such as phone, gas and electricity.

How to Fill In Clause 9:

In the blank, fill in the utilities you—not the tenants—will be responsible for paying. If you will not be paying for any utilities, simply write in "N/A" or "Not Applicable."

Disclose Shared Utility Arrangements

If there are not separate gas and electric meters for each unit, or a tenant's meter serves any areas outside his unit (such as a water heater used in common with other tenants or even a light bulb not under the tenant's control in a common area), you should disclose this in your lease or rental agreement. Simply add details to Clause 9. This type of disclosure is required by law in some states, and is only fair in any case. The best solution is to put in a separate meter for the areas served outside the tenant's unit. If you don't do that, you should:

- pay for the utilities for the tenant's meter yourself by placing that utility in your name
- reduce the tenant's rent to compensate for payment of utility usage outside of her unit (this will probably cost you more in the long run than if you either added a new meter or simply paid for the utilities yourself), or
- sign a separate written agreement with the tenant, under which the tenant specifically agrees to pay for others' utilities too.

Clause 10. Assignment and Subletting

Tenant will not sublet any part of the premises or assign this Agreement without the prior written consent of Landlord.

Clause 10 is an anti-subletting clause, breach of which is grounds for eviction. It prevents a tenant from subleasing during a vacation or renting out a room to someone unless you specifically agree.

Clause 10 is also designed to prevent assignments, a legal term that means your tenant transfers her tenancy to someone else. Practically, you need this clause to prevent your tenant from leaving in the middle of the month or lease term and moving in a replacement—maybe someone you wouldn't choose to rent to—without your consent.

By including Clause 10 in your lease or rental agreement, you have the option not to accept the person your tenant proposes to take over the lease. Under the law of most states, however, you should realize that if a tenant who wishes to leave early provides you with another suitable tenant, you can't both unreasonably refuse to rent to this person and hold the tenant financially liable for breaking the lease. Typically, state law requires that you must try to re-rent the property reasonably quickly and subtract any rent you receive from the amount the original tenant owed you for the remainder of the agreed-upon rental period. Lawyers call this the mitigation-of-damages rule, a bit of legalese it's valuable to know.

Common Terms

Tenant. Someone who has signed a lease or a rental agreement, or who has gained the status of a tenant because the landlord has accepted his presence on the property or has accepted rent from him.

Cotenants. Two or more tenants who rent the same property under the same lease or rental agreement, each 100% responsible for carrying out the agreement, including paying all the rent.

Subtenant. Someone who subleases (rents) all or part of the premises from a tenant and does not sign a lease or rental agreement with the landlord. A subtenant may either rent (sublet) an entire dwelling from a tenant who moves out temporarily—for example, for the summer—or rent one or more rooms from the tenant who continues to live in the unit. The key to subtenant relationships is that the original tenant retains the primary relationship with the landlord and continues to exercise some control over the rental property, either by occupying part of the unit or by reserving the right to retake possession at a later date.

Assignment. The transfer by a tenant of all of his rights of tenancy to another tenant (the "assignee"). Unlike a subtenant, an assignee rents directly from the landlord.

Roommates. Two or more people, usually unrelated, living under the same roof and sharing rent and expenses. A roommate is usually a cotenant, but in some situations may be a subtenant.

Should You Allow a Sublet or Assignment?

As a general rule, your best bet when a tenant asks to sublease or assign is to simply insist that the tenancy terminate and a new one begin—with the proposed "subtenant" or "assignee" as the new tenant, after signing a new lease or rental agreement. This gives you the most direct legal relationship with the substitute. There are a few situations, however, in which you may want to agree to a subtenancy or assignment.

You might, for example, want to accommodate—and keep—an exceptional, long-term tenant who has every intention of returning and whose judgment and integrity you have always trusted. If the proposed stand-in meets your normal tenant criteria, you may decide that it is worth the risk of a subtenancy or assignment in order to keep the original tenant.

Another good reason is a desire to have a sure source of funds in the background. This might come up if your original tenant is financially sound and trustworthy, but a proposed stand-in is less secure but acceptable in every other respect. By agreeing to a sublet or assignment, you have someone in the background (the original tenant) still responsible for the rent. The risk you incur by agreeing to set up a subtenancy or assignment and the hassle that comes with dealing with more than one person may be worth what you gain in keeping a sure and reliable source of funds on the hook.

How to Fill In Clause 10:

You don't need to add anything to this clause.

For a related discussion of subleases, assignments and the landlord's duty to mitigate damages, see Chapter 5, Section C. Also, Chapter 8 of Every Landlord's Legal Guide, *by Marcia Stewart, Ralph Warner and Janet Portman (Nolo Press) covers these topics in detail.*

Clause 11. Tenant's Maintenance Responsibilities

Tenant will: (1) keep the premises clean, sanitary and in good condition and, upon termination of the tenancy, return the premises to Landlord in a condition identical to that which existed when Tenant took occupancy, except for ordinary wear and tear; (2) immediately notify Landlord of any defects or dangerous conditions in and about the premises of which Tenant becomes aware; and (3) reimburse Landlord, on demand by Landlord, for the cost of any repairs to the premises damaged by Tenant or Tenant's guests or business invitees through misuse or neglect.

Tenant has examined the premises, including appliances, fixtures, carpets, drapes and paint, and has found them to be in good, safe and clean condition and repair, except as noted in the Landlord/Tenant Checklist.

Clause 11 makes the tenant responsible for keeping the rental premises clean and sanitary. This clause also makes it clear that if the tenant damages the premises—for example, by breaking a window or scratching hardwood floors—it's his responsibility to pay for the damage.

It is the law in some states (and a wise practice in all) to notify tenants in writing of procedures for making complaint and repair requests. Clause 11 requires the tenant to alert you to defective or dangerous conditions. LeaseWriter includes forms for handling repair requests and responses, and filled-in samples are shown in Chapter 4 of this book.

Before the tenant moves in, you and the tenant should inspect the rental unit and fill out the Landlord/Tenant Checklist in Chapter 4, describing what is in the unit and noting any problems. Doing so will help you avoid disputes over security deposit deductions when the tenant moves out.

How to Fill In Clause 11:

You do not need to add anything to this clause.

Avoid Problems by Adopting a Good Maintenance and Repair System

As a general rule, you are legally required to offer livable premises when a tenant originally rents an apartment or rental unit and to maintain the premises throughout the rental term. If rental property is not kept in good repair, the tenant may have the right to repair the problem and deduct the cost from the rent, withhold rent, sue for any injuries caused by defective conditions or move out without notice. Your best defense against rent-withholding hassles and other disputes with tenants is to establish and communicate a clear, easy-to-follow procedure for tenants to ask for repairs and for you to document all complaints, respond quickly when complaints are made and schedule annual safety inspections. And, if you employ a manager or management company, make sure she or it fully accepts and implements your guidelines. Follow these steps to avoid maintenance and repair problems with tenants:

1. Regularly look for dangerous conditions on the property and fix them promptly. Reduce risk exposure as much as possible—for example, by providing sufficient lighting in hallways, parking garages and other common areas, strong locks on doors and windows and safe stairs and handrails.

2. Scrupulously comply with all public health and safety codes. Your local building or housing authority, and health or fire department, can provide any information you need. Also, check state housing laws governing landlords' repair and maintenance responsibilities. (The 50-State Law Browser includes citations for the major state laws affecting landlords. Check your statutes under headings such as Landlord Obligations to Maintain Premises.)

3. Clearly set out your and the tenant's responsibilities for repair and maintenance in your lease or rental agreement. (See Clauses 11, 12 and 13 of the agreements in this chapter.)

4. Use the written Landlord/Tenant Checklist form in Chapter 4 to check over the premises and fix any problems before new tenants move in.

5. Encourage tenants to immediately report plumbing, heating, weatherproofing or other defects and safety or security problems—whether in the tenant's unit or in common areas such as hallways and parking garages. The Maintenance/Repair Request form shown in Chapter 4 is useful for this purpose.

6. Handle repairs (especially urgent ones, such as a broken door lock or lack of heat in winter) as soon as possible. Notify the tenant by phone and follow up in writing if repairs will take more than 48 hours, excluding weekends. Keep the tenant informed—for example, if you have problems scheduling a plumber, let your tenant know with a phone call or a note. For nonurgent repairs, be sure to give the tenant proper notice as required by state law. (See Clause 15 for details on notice required to enter rental premises.)

7. Keep a written log of all tenant complaints, including those made orally. Record your immediate and any follow-up responses (and subsequent tenant communications) and details as to how and when the problem was fixed, including reasons for any delay. The Maintenance/Repair Request form shown in Chapter 4 is useful for this purpose.

8. Twice a year, give your tenants a checklist on which to report any potential safety hazards or problems that might have been overlooked—for example, low water pressure in the shower, peeling paint or noisy neighbors. This is also a good time to remind tenants of their repair and maintenance responsibilities. Respond promptly and in writing to all repair requests, keeping copies in your file.

9. Once a year, inspect all rental units for safety and maintenance problems. Make sure smoke detectors, heating and plumbing systems and major appliances are in fact safe and in good working order.

10. Get a good liability insurance policy to cover injuries or losses suffered by others as the result of defective conditions on the property and lawyers' bills for defending personal injury suits.

Renter's Insurance

It is becoming increasingly popular, especially in high-end rentals, to require tenants to obtain renter's insurance. It covers losses to the tenant's belongings as a result of fire or theft. Often called a "Tenant's Package Policy," renter's insurance also covers the tenant if his negligence causes injury to other people or property damage (to his property or to yours). Besides protecting the tenant from personal liability, renter's insurance benefits you, too: If damage caused by the tenant could be covered by either his insurance policy or yours—for example, the tenant starts a fire when he leaves the stove on—a claim made on the tenant's policy will affect his premiums, not yours.

If you decide to require insurance, insert a clause like the following at the end of your lease or rental agreement, under Clause 22, Additional Provisions. This will help assure that the tenant purchases and maintains a renter's insurance policy throughout his tenancy.

Renter's Insurance

Within ten days of the signing of this Agreement, Tenant will obtain renter's insurance and provide proof of purchase to Landlord. Tenant further agrees to maintain the policy throughout the duration of the tenancy, and to furnish proof of insurance on a ☐ yearly ☐ semi-annual basis.

Several times in this book, we recommend Every Landlord's Legal Guide *by Marcia Stewart, Ralph Warner and Janet Portman (Nolo Press). It is especially useful for its detailed discussion of landlords' and tenants' rights and responsibilities for repair and maintenance under state and local laws and judicial decisions. It provides practical advice on how to stay on top of repair and maintenance needs and minimize financial losses and legal problems with tenants. It discusses tenants' rights if you do not meet your legal responsibilities and the pros and cons of delegating repairs and maintenance to the tenant.* Every Landlord's Legal Guide *also includes chapters on landlord's liability for tenant injuries from defective housing conditions, such as a broken step or defective wiring, liability for environmental hazards such as asbestos and lead, and landlord's responsibility to provide secure premises and protect tenants from assault or criminal activities, such as drug dealing.*

Clause 12. Repairs and Alterations by Tenant

a. Except as provided by law or as authorized by the prior written consent of Landlord, Tenant will not make any repairs or alterations to the premises, including nailing holes in the walls or painting the rental unit.

b. Tenant will not, without Landlord's prior written consent, alter, re-key or install any locks to the premises or install or alter any burglar alarm system. Tenant will provide Landlord with a key or keys capable of unlocking all such re-keyed or new locks as well as instructions on how to disarm any altered or new burglar alarm system

Clause 12 makes it clear that the tenant may not make alterations and repairs without your consent, including painting or nailing holes in the walls.

And to make sure you can take advantage of your legal right of entry in an emergency situation, Clause 12 specifically forbids the tenant from re-keying the locks or installing a burglar alarm system without your consent. If you do grant permission, make sure your tenant gives you duplicate keys or the name and phone number of the alarm company or instructions on how to disarm the alarm system so that you can enter in case of emergency.

The "except as provided by law" language in Clause 12 is a reference to the fact that, in certain situations and in certain states, tenants have a narrowly defined right to alter or repair the premises, regardless of what you've said in the lease or rental agreement. Examples include:

- **Alterations by a disabled person, such as lowering counter tops for a wheelchair-bound tenant.** Under the Federal Fair Housing Act, a disabled person may modify her living space to the extent necessary to make the space safe and comfortable, as long as the modifications will not make the unit unacceptable to the next tenant, or if the disabled tenant agrees to undo the modification when she leaves. (42 U.S.Code §3604(f)(3)(A).)

- **Use of the "repair and deduct" procedure.** In most states, tenants have the right to repair defects or damage that make the premises uninhabitable or substantially interfere with the tenant's safe use or enjoyment of the premises. Usually, the tenant must first notify you of the problem and give you a reasonable amount of time to fix it.

- **Specific alterations allowed by state statutes.** Some states allow tenants to install energy conservation measures (like removable interior storm windows), or burglary prevention devices, without the landlord's prior consent. Check your state statutes or call your local rental property association for more information on these types of laws.

How to Fill In Clause 12:

If you do not want the tenant to make any repairs without your permission, you do not need to add anything to this clause.

You may, however, want to go further and specifically prohibit certain repairs or alterations by adding details in Clause 22 (Additional Provisions). For example, you may want to make it clear that any "fixtures"—a legal term that describes any addition that is attached to the structure, such as bolted-in bookcases or built-in dishwashers—are your property and may not be removed by the tenant without your permission.

If you do authorize the tenant to make any repairs, provide enough detail so that the tenant knows exactly what is expected, how much repairs can cost and who will pay. For example, if you decide to allow the tenant to take over the repair of any broken windows, routine plumbing jobs or landscaping, give specific descriptions and limits to the tasks.

⚠️ ***Do not delegate to a tenant your responsibility for major maintenance of essential services.***
The duty to repair and maintain heating, plumbing and electrical and structural systems (the roof, for example) is yours. Absent unusual circumstances, and even then only after carefully checking state law, it's a mistake to try to delegate this responsibility to the tenant. Many courts have held that landlords cannot delegate to a tenant the responsibility for keeping the premises fit for habitation, fearing that the tenant will rarely be in the position, either practically or financially, to do the kinds of repairs that are often needed to bring a structure up to par.

Clause 13. Violating Laws and Causing Disturbances

Tenant is entitled to quiet enjoyment of the premises. Tenant and guests or invitees will not use the premises or adjacent areas in such a way as to: (1) violate any law or ordinance, including laws prohibiting the use, possession or sale of illegal drugs; (2) commit waste (severe property damage); or (3) create a nuisance by annoying, disturbing, inconveniencing or interfering with the quiet enjoyment and peace and quiet of any other tenant or nearby resident.

This type of clause is found in most form leases and rental agreements. Although it contains some legal jargon, it's probably best to leave it as is, since courts have much experience in working with these terms. As courts define it, the "covenant of quiet enjoyment" amounts to an implied promise that you will not act (or fail to act) in a way that interferes with or destroys the ability of the tenant to use the rented premises.

Examples of violations of the covenant of quiet enjoyment include:

- allowing garbage to pile up
- tolerating a major rodent infestation, or
- failing to control a tenant whose constant loud music makes it impossible for other tenants to sleep.

If you want more specific rules—for example, no loud music played after midnight—add them to Clause 18: Rules and Regulations, or to Clause 22: Additional Provisions.

How to Fill In Clause 13:

You do not need to add anything to this clause.

Waste and Nuisance: What Are They?

In legalese, committing **waste** means causing severe damage to real estate, including a house or an apartment unit—damage that goes way beyond ordinary wear and tear. Punching holes in walls, pulling out sinks and fixtures and knocking down doors are examples of waste.

Nuisance means behavior that prevents neighbors from fully enjoying the use of their homes. Continuous loud noise and foul odors are examples of legal nuisances that may disturb nearby neighbors. So, too, are selling drugs or engaging in other illegal activities that greatly disturb neighbors.

How to Prevent Illegal Tenant Activity

There are several practical steps you can take both to avoid trouble among your tenants and, in the event that hostilities do erupt, to limit your exposure to lawsuits:

- Screen tenants carefully and choose tenants who are likely to be law-abiding and peaceful citizens. (Chapter 3 recommends a comprehensive system for screening prospective tenants, including checking out references from past landlords and employers.)
- Establish a system to respond to tenants' complaints and concerns about other tenants, especially those involving drug dealing on the rental property.
- Make it clear that you will not tolerate tenants' disruptive behavior. An explicit lease or rental agreement provision such as Clause 13 prohibiting drug dealing and illegal activity is the most effective way to make this point. If a tenant does cause trouble, act swiftly. Some situations, such as drug dealing, call for prompt efforts to evict the troublemaker. Your failure to evict drug-dealing tenants can result in lawsuits from tenants injured or annoyed by drug dealers, and local, state or federal authorities may choose to levy stiff fines for allowing the illegal activity to continue. In extreme cases, you may actually lose your property to the government under public nuisance abatement laws and forfeiture laws.

Clause 14. Pets

No animal, bird or other pet will be kept on the premises, even temporarily, except properly trained dogs needed by blind, deaf or disabled persons and _____

_____.

under the following conditions:

_____

_____

This clause is designed to prevent tenants from keeping pets without your written permission. This is not necessarily to say that you will want to apply a flat "no-pets" rule. (Many landlords, in fact, report that pet-owning tenants are more appreciative, stable and responsible than the norm.) But it does provide you with a legal mechanism designed to keep your premises from being waist-deep in Irish wolfhounds. Without this sort of provision, particularly if you use a longer-term lease that can't be terminated early save for a clear violation of one of its provisions, there's little to prevent your tenant from keeping dangerous or nonhousebroken pets on your property, except for city ordinances prohibiting tigers and the like.

You have the right to prohibit all pets, or to restrict the types of pets you allow, with the exception of trained dogs used by blind, deaf or physically or mentally disabled people.

How to Fill In Clause 14:

If you do not allow pets, put the word "None" in the blanks.

If you allow pets, be sure to identify the type and number of pets in the first blank—for example, "one cat" or "one dog under 20 pounds." It's also wise to spell out your pet rules in the second blank—for example, you may want to specify that the tenants will keep the yard free of all animal waste. (Your Rules and Regulations may be another place to do this. See Clause 18.)

Renting to Pet Owners

Project Open Door, an ambitious program of the San Francisco Society for the Prevention of Cruelty to Animals (SPCA), seeks to show landlords how to make renting to pet-owning tenants a satisfying and profitable experience. The SPCA offers landlords:

- checklists to help screen pet-owning tenants
- pet policies to add to standard leases and rental agreements, and
- free mediation if landlords and tenants have pet-related problems after moving in.

For more information, contact the San Francisco SPCA at 2500 16th St., San Francisco, CA 94103, 415-554-3000. Also, see *Dog Law*, by Mary Randolph (Nolo Press) for more information on renting to pet owners.

Should You Require a Separate Security Deposit for Pets?

Some landlords allow pets but require the tenant to pay a separate deposit to cover any damages caused by the pet. The laws of a few states specifically allow separate, nonrefundable pet deposits. In others, charging a designated pet deposit is legal only if the total amount you charge for deposits does not exceed the state maximum for all deposits. (See Clause 8 for details on security deposits.)

Even where allowed, separate pet deposits can often be a bad idea because they limit how you can use that part of the security deposit. For example, if the pet is well behaved, but the tenant trashes your unit, you can't use the pet portion of the deposit to clean up after the human. If you want to protect your property from damage done by a pet, you are probably better off charging a slightly higher rent or security deposit to start with (assuming you are not restricted by rent control or the upper security deposit limits).

⚠️ *It is illegal to charge an extra pet deposit for people with trained guide dogs, signal dogs or service dogs.*

Clause 15. Landlord's Right to Access

Landlord or Landlord's agents may enter the premises in the event of an emergency, to make repairs or improvements or to show the premises to prospective buyers or tenants. Landlord may also enter the premises to conduct an annual inspection to check for safety or maintenance problems. Except in cases of emergency, Tenant's abandonment of the premises, court order, or where it is impractical to do so, Landlord shall give Tenant _____ notice before entering.

The tenant's duty to pay rent is typically conditioned on your having fulfilled your legal responsibility to properly repair and maintain the premises. This means that, of necessity, you have a legal responsibility to keep fairly close tabs on the condition of the property. For this reason, and because it makes good sense to allow landlords reasonable access to their property, nearly every state clearly recognizes the right of a landlord to legally enter rented premises while a tenant is still in residence, under certain broad circumstances, such as to deal with an emergency and when the tenant gives permission.

About half the states have access laws specifying the circumstances under which landlords may legally enter rented premises. Most access laws allow landlords to enter rental units to make repairs and inspect the property and to show property to prospective tenants. (See "General Rules of Entry," below.) State access laws typically specify the amount of notice required for such entry—usually 24 hours (unless it is impractical to do so—for example, in

cases of emergency). A few states simply require the landlord to provide "reasonable" notice, often presumed to be 24 hours.

Clause 15 makes it clear to the tenant that
you have a legal right of access to the property
to make repairs or to show the premises for
sale or rental, provided you give the tenant reasonable notice. (The 50-State Law Browser
provides details on a landlord's right to entry
and notice requirements.) LeaseWriter includes
a Notice of Intent to Enter Dwelling Unit form

and a filled-in sample is shown in Chapter 4 of
this book.

How to Fill In Clause 15:

In the blank, indicate the amount of notice
you will provide the tenant before entering,
at least the minimum required in your state.
If your state law simply requires "reasonable"
notice or has no notice requirement, we suggest you provide at least 24 hours' notice.

General Rules of Entry

Here are the general circumstances under
which landlords may legally enter rented
premises. Except in cases of emergency, or
where it is impractical to do so, you generally must enter only at reasonable times and
you must give at least the amount and type
of notice required in your state.

Emergency. In all states, you can enter
rental property to respond to a true emergency—such as a gas leak.

**To make repairs or inspect the
property.** By law, many states allow you
and your repairperson to enter the tenant's
home to make necessary or agreed-upon
repairs, decorations, alterations or improvements and to supply necessary or agreed-
upon services—for example, when you need
to fix a broken oven.

To show property. Most states with
access laws allow a landlord to enter rented

property to show it to prospective tenants
toward the end of the tenancy or to prospective purchasers if the landlord wishes
to sell the property. (See Chapter 3, Section B, for advice on renting property
that's still occupied.)

**With the permission of the ten-
ant.** You can always enter rental property,
even without notice, if the tenant agrees.

**Entry after the tenant has
moved out.** To state the obvious, you
may enter the premises after the tenant
has completely moved out—regardless of
whether the tenant left voluntarily after
giving back the key, or involuntarily, as a
result of an eviction lawsuit. In addition,
if you believe the tenant has abandoned
the property—that is, skipped out without giving any notice or returning the
key—you may legally enter.

Clause 16. Extended Absences by Tenant

Tenant will notify Landlord in advance if Tenant will be away from the premises for _____ or more consecutive days. During such absence, Landlord may enter the premises at times reasonably necessary to maintain the property and inspect for needed repairs.

Several states with statutes that otherwise protect a tenant's privacy by requiring notice before entry (except in case of emergency) give landlords the specific legal right to enter the rental unit during a tenant's extended absence to maintain the property as necessary and to inspect for damage and needed repairs. Extended absence is often defined as seven days or more. For cxample, if you live in a cold-weather place and temperatures take a dive, it makes sense to check the pipes in rental units (to make sure they haven't burst) when the tenant is away for winter vacation.

While many states do not address this issue, you should be on safe legal ground to enter rental property during a tenant's extended absence, as long as you have a genuine reason to enter to protect the property from damage. You should enter only if something really needs to be done—that is, something the tenant would do if he were home, as part of his obligation to keep the property clean, safe and in good repair.

To protect yourself, include Clause 16, which requires that the tenants notify you when leaving your property for an extended time and alerts the tenant of your intent to enter the premises during these times if necessary.

How to Fill In Clause 16:

In the blank, fill in the time frame that you think is reasonable. Ten or 14 days is common.

Clause 17. Possession of the Premises

a. *Tenant's failure to take possession.*
   If, after signing this Agreement, Tenant fails to take possession of the premises, Tenant will still be responsible for paying rent and complying with all other terms of this Agreement.

b. *Landlord's failure to deliver possession.*
   If Landlord is unable to deliver possession of the premises to Tenant for any reason not within Landlord's control, including, but not limited to, partial or complete destruction of the premises, Tenant will have the right to terminate this Agreement upon proper notice as required by law. In such event, Landlord's liability to Tenant will be limited to the return of all sums previously paid by Tenant to Landlord.

The first part of this clause (part a) explains that a tenant who chooses not to move in after signing the lease or rental agreement will still be required to pay rent and satisfy other conditions of the agreement. This does not mean, however, that you can sit back and expect to collect rent for the entire lease or rental agreement term. (As we explain in Chapter 5, you generally must take reasonably prompt steps to re-rent the premises, and you must credit the rent you collect against the first tenant's rent obligation.)

The second part of the clause (part b) protects you if you're unable, for reasons beyond your control, to turn over possession after having signed the agreement or lease—for example, if a fire spreads from next door and destroys the premises. It limits your financial liability to the new tenant to the return of any prepaid rent and security deposits (the "sums previously paid" in the language of the clause).

⚠ **Clause 17 may not limit your liability if you cannot deliver possession because the old tenant is still on the premises—even if he is the subject of an eviction that you ultimately win.** *When a holdover tenant prevents the new tenant from moving in, landlords are often sued by the new tenant for not only the return of any prepaid rent and security deposits, but also the costs of temporary housing, storage costs and other losses. In some states, an attempt in the lease to limit the new tenant's recovery to the return of prepaid sums alone would not hold up in court. To protect yourself, you will want to shift some of the financial liability to the holdover tenant. You'll have a stronger chance of doing this if the old tenant has given written notice of his intent to move out. (See Clause 4, above, which requires written notice.)*

How to Fill In Clause 17:

You do not need to add anything to this clause.

Clause 18. Tenant Rules and Regulations

☐ Tenant acknowledges receipt of, and has read a copy of, tenant rules and regulations, which are attached to and incorporated into this Agreement by this reference.

Many landlords don't worry about detailed rules and regulations, especially when they rent single-family homes or duplexes. However, in larger buildings with many tenants, rules are usually important to control the use of common areas and equipment—both for the convenience, safety and welfare of the tenants and as a way to protect your property from damage. Rules and regulations also help avoid confusion and misunderstandings about day-to-day issues such as garbage disposal.

Not every minor rule needs to be incorporated in your lease or rental agreement. But it is a good idea to specifically incorporate important ones (especially those that are likely to be ignored by some tenants). Doing so gives you the authority to evict a tenant who persists in seriously violating your code of tenant rules and regulations. Also, to avoid charges of illegal discrimination, rules and regulations should apply equally to all tenants in your rental property.

Because tenant rules and regulations are often lengthy and may be revised occasionally, we suggest you prepare a separate attachment. Be sure the rules and regulations (including any revisions) are dated on each page and signed by both you and the tenant.

How to Fill In Clause 18:

If you have a set of Tenant Rules and Regulations, check the box. If you do not, simply put a line through this clause or write the words "N/A" or "Not Applicable."

What's Covered in Tenant Rules and Regulations

Tenant rules and regulations typically cover issues such as:

- elevator safety and use
- pool rules
- garbage disposal and recycling
- vehicles and parking regulations—for example, restrictions of repairs on the premises or types of vehicles (such as no RVs)
- lock-out and lost key charges
- pet rules
- no smoking in common areas
- security system use
- specific details on what's considered excessive noise
- dangerous materials—nothing explosive should be on the premises
- storage of bikes, baby strollers and other equipment in halls, stairways and other common areas
- specific landlord and tenant maintenance responsibilities (such as stopped-up toilets or garbage disposals, broken windows, rodent and pest control, lawn and yard maintenance)
- use of the grounds and recreation areas
- maintenance of balconies and decks (for instance, no drying clothes on balconies)
- display of signs in windows
- laundry room rules
- waterbeds.

Clause 19. Payment of Court Costs and Attorney Fees in a Lawsuit

In any action or legal proceeding to enforce any part of this Agreement, the prevailing party ☐ shall not/ ☐ shall recover reasonable attorney fees and court costs.

Many landlords assume that if they sue a tenant and win, the court will order the losing tenant to pay the landlord's court costs (filing fees, service of process charges, deposition costs and so on) and attorney fees. This is not generally true. In most states, a court will order the losing tenant to pay your attorney fees only if a written agreement specifically provides for it.

If, however, you have an "attorney fees" clause in your lease, all this changes. If you hire a lawyer to bring a lawsuit and win, the judge will order your tenant to pay your costs and attorney fees. (In rare instances, a court will order the loser to pay costs and fees on its own if it finds that the behavior of the losing party was particularly egregious.)

But there's another important issue you need to know about. By law in many states, an attorney-fees clause in a lease or a rental agreement works both ways, even if you haven't written it that way. That is, even if the lease states only that you are entitled to attorney fees if you win a lawsuit, your tenants will be entitled to collect their attorney fees from you if they prevail. The amount you would be ordered to pay would be whatever the judge decides is reasonable.

So, especially if you live in a state that will read a "one-way" attorney-fees clause as a two-way street, give some thought to whether you want to bind both of you to paying for the winner's costs and fees. Remember, if you can't actually collect a judgment containing attorney fees from an evicted tenant (which often happens), the clause will not help you. But if the tenant prevails, you will be stuck paying his costs and fees. In addition, the presence of a two-way clause will make it far easier for a tenant to secure a willing lawyer for even a doubtful claim, because the source of the lawyer's fee (you, if you lose) will probably appear more financially solid than if the client were paying the bill himself.

Especially if you intend to do all or most of your own legal work in any potential eviction or other lawsuit, you will almost surely be better off not to allow for attorney fees. Why? Because if the tenant wins, you will have to pay her fees; but if you win, she will owe you nothing since you didn't hire an attorney. You can't even recover for the long hours you spent preparing for and handling the case.

Finally, be aware that attorney-fees clauses only cover lawsuits concerning the meaning or implementation of the lease—such as a dispute about rent, security deposits or your right to access. An attorney-fees clause would not apply in a personal injury or discrimination lawsuit.

How to Fill In Clause 19:

If you don't want to allow for attorney fees, check the box before the words "shall not" and cross out the word "shall."

If you want to be entitled to attorney fees and costs if you win—and you're willing to pay them if you lose—check the box before the word "shall" and cross out the words "shall not."

Clause 20. Disclosures

Tenant acknowledges that Landlord has made the following disclosures regarding the premises:

☐ Disclosure of Information on Lead-Based Paint and/or Lead-Based Paint Hazards

☐ Other disclosures:

_____

_____

_____

Federal, state or local laws may require you to make certain disclosures before a new tenant signs a lease or rental agreement or moves in.

Lead Disclosures

If your rental unit was built prior to 1978, before signing a lease or rental agreement, you must tell new tenants about any known lead-based paint or lead-based paint hazards in the rental premises. You must also give them an EPA pamphlet, *Protect Your Family From Lead in Your Home.* This is a requirement of the Residential Lead-Based Paint Hazard Reduction Act, commonly known as Title X (42 U.S. Code 4852d), which is administered by the U.S. Environmental Protection Agency (EPA).

In addition, both you and the tenant must sign an EPA-approved form—Disclosure of Information on Lead-Based Paint and/or Lead-Based Paint Hazards—that will prove that you told your tenants what you know about these hazards on your premises. You must keep the disclosure form as part of your records for three years from the date of the start of the tenancy.

As discussed below, state laws on lead disclosure may also come into play.

LeaseWriter includes the Disclosure of Information on Lead-Based Paint and/or Lead-Based Paint Hazards form, and a sample is shown at the end of this chapter.

Penalties are severe.
Property owners who fail to comply with EPA regulations for disclosing lead-based paint hazards face penalties of up to $10,000 for each violation and treble (triple) damages if a tenant is injured by your willful noncompliance.

Rental Properties Exempt From Title X Regulations

- Housing built after January 1978
- housing certified lead-free by an accredited lead inspector
- lofts, efficiencies and studios
- short-term vacation rentals
- a single room rented in a residential dwelling
- housing designed for persons with disabilities, unless children under age six are present
- retirement communities (housing designed for seniors, where one or more tenant is at least 62 years old), unless children under age six are present.

Resources: Lead

Copies of Title X regulations and background information may be obtained by calling the National Lead Information Center at 800-424-LEAD, or checking its Website: www.nsc.org/ehc/lead.htm. Information on the evaluation and control of lead may be obtained from the regional offices of the EPA, or the EPA Web site: www.epa.gov.

Some states require property owners to disclose lead hazards to prospective tenants. The 50-State Law Browser includes information on state lead hazard laws. If a state statute is more protective of the tenant than the federal standard under Title X, you must follow the state statute. Alternatively, your state may choose to develop its own form, as long as it is consistent with the EPA model. Check with your state housing department or local office of the U.S. Department of Housing and Urban Development (HUD) to find out if this applies to you.

Disclosures of Hidden Defects

If there is any hidden (not obvious) aspect of your property that could cause injury or substantially interfere with a tenant's safe enjoyment and use of the dwelling—for example, an elevator that may be dangerous—your best bet is to fix it. If this is impossible, you are likely to be better off legally (should a future problem develop) if you disclose the defective condition before the tenant signs the lease or rental agreement. While disclosure doesn't guarantee that you won't be legally liable (also make sure your insurance protects you), it will likely help. Putting the tenant on notice that a problem exists will help prevent injuries and limit your liability should an injury occur from a defective condition in the rental unit or on the premises.

One example of a sensible disclosure would be warning the tenant that the building contains asbestos insulation that is not believed to be a problem because it is sealed inside walls, but could be dangerous if the tenant or anyone

else makes a hole in the wall. Another sensible disclosure might be to tell the tenant that your building is in an urban neighborhood where criminal acts are known to occur (or even that there have been criminal acts on your property), and that given this knowledge, it is your tenant's responsibility to conduct himself appropriately. Or, if an open parking lot is sometimes icy, and you don't sand it, your tenants should be put on notice.

If you have a question about whether to disclose a particular fact about the premises, resolve it in favor of disclosure in order to limit liability (should a tenant or guest be injured by the defect). This is also just a good way to ensure positive landlord-tenant relations.

 Some problems need to be fixed, not merely disclosed.
Warning your tenants about a hidden defect does not absolve you of legal responsibility if the condition makes the dwelling uninhabitable or unreasonably dangerous. For example, you are courting liability if you rent an apartment with a gas heater that you know might blow up, even if you warn the tenant that the heater is faulty. Nor can you simply warn your tenants about prior crime on the premises and then fail to do anything (like installing deadbolts or hiring security) to promote safety.

Other Disclosures

State laws may impose disclosure requirements, too, such as the need to inform tenants of the name and address of the bank where their security deposit is held. (Clause 8 covers security deposits.) Local rent control ordinances often require disclosures such as the name and address of the government agency or elected board that administers the ordinance. Check your state and local laws for details on disclosure requirements.

How to Fill In Clause 20:

If your rental property was built before 1978, you must meet federal lead disclosure requirements, so check the first box, and follow the advice above.

If you are legally required to make other disclosures as described above, check the second box and provide details in the blank space, adding additional pages as necessary.

Clause 21. Authority to Receive Legal Papers

The Landlord, any person managing the premises and anyone designated by the Landlord are authorized to accept service of process and receive other notices and demands, which may be delivered to:

☐ The Landlord, at the following address:

_____

_____

☐ The manager, at the following address:

_____

_____

☐ The following person, at the following address:

_____

_____

It's the law in many states, and a good idea in all, to give your tenants information about everyone whom you have authorized to receive notices and legal papers, such as a tenant's notice that she is ending the tenancy or a tenant's court documents as part of an eviction defense. Of course, you may want to handle all of this yourself or delegate it to a manager or management company. Make sure the person you designate to receive legal papers is almost always available to receive tenant notices and legal papers. Also, be sure to keep your tenants up to date on any changes in this information.

How to Fill In Clause 21:

Provide your name and street address or the name and address of someone else you authorize to receive notices and legal papers on your behalf, such as a property manager.

Clause 22.   Additional Provisions

Additional provisions are as follows:_____

_____

In this clause, you may list any additional provisions or agreements that are unique to you and the particular tenant signing the lease or rental agreement. We recommend that you scrupulously record all extra details in order to avoid disputes with tenants. Here's a good example of the kind of details you should include as an additional provision:

EXAMPLE: Landlord will supply up to $150 worth of paint and painting supplies. Tenant will paint the living room, hall and two bedrooms, using off-white latex paint on the walls and water-based enamel on all wood surfaces (doors and trim). Paint and supplies shall be picked up by Tenant from ABC Hardware and billed to Landlord.

If you don't have a separate Rules and Regulations clause (see Clause 18, above), you may spell out a few rules under this clause—for example, regarding lost key charges or use of a pool on the property.

How to Fill In Clause 22:

List additional provisions or rules here or in an attachment. If there are no additional provisions, write "N/A" or "Not Applicable."

There is no legal or practical imperative to put every small detail you want to communicate to the tenant into your lease or rental agreement.
Instead, prepare a welcoming, but no-nonsense "move-in letter" that dovetails with the lease or rental agreement and highlights important terms of the tenancy—for example, how and where to report maintenance problems. You may also use a move-in letter to cover issues not included in the lease or rental agreement—for example, rules for use of a laundry room. (Chapter 4 covers move-in letters.)

Do not include exculpatory ("If there's a problem, I'm not responsible") clauses or hold harmless ("If there's a problem, you are responsible") clauses.
Many form leases include provisions that attempt to absolve you in advance from responsibility for your legal misdeeds. For example, one lease form generated by a popular software package contains a broad provision stating that you are not responsible for injuries to tenants and guests, even those you cause intentionally. Such nonsense is blatantly illegal—if you beat up your tenant, no boilerplate lease provision will protect you from civil and probably criminal charges. These clauses make you seem like an ogre at the same time they do you no practical good.

Clause 23. Validity of Each Part

If any portion of this Agreement is held to be invalid, its invalidity will not affect the validity or enforceability of any other provision of this Agreement.

This clause is known as a "savings" clause, and it is commonly used in contracts. It means that, in the unlikely event that one of the other clauses in the Agreement is found to be invalid by a court, the remainder of the Agreement will remain in force.

How to Fill In Clause 23:

You do not need to add anything to this clause.

Clause 24. Grounds for Termination of Tenancy

The failure of Tenant or Tenant's guests or invitees to comply with any term of this Agreement is grounds for termination of the tenancy, with appropriate notice to Tenant and procedures as required by law.

This clause states that any violation of the Agreement by the tenant, or by the tenant's business or social guests, is grounds for terminating the tenancy, according to the procedures established by your state or local laws. Making the tenant responsible for the actions of his guests can be extremely important—for example, if you discover that the tenant's family or friends are using or dealing illegal drugs on the premises or have damaged the property.

How to Fill In Clause 24:

You do not need to add anything to this clause.

Clause 25. Entire Agreement

This document constitutes the entire Agreement between the parties, and no promises or representations, other than those contained here and those implied by law, have been made by Landlord or Tenant. Any modifications to this Agreement must be in writing signed by Landlord and Tenant.

This clause establishes that the lease or rental agreement and any attachments (such as Rules and Regulations) constitute the entire agreement between you and your tenant. It means that oral promises (by you or the tenant) to do something different with respect to any aspect of the rental are not binding. Any changes or additions must be in writing. (Chapter 5, Section A, discusses how to modify signed rental agreements and leases.)

How to Fill In Clause 25:

You do not need to add anything to this clause.

C. Signing the Lease or Rental Agreement

At the end of the lease or rental agreement, there's space to include your signature, street address and phone number, or that of the person you authorize as your agent, such as a property manager. There's also space for the tenants' signatures and phone numbers.

If the tenant has a cosigner (discussed, below), you'll need to add a line for the cosigner's signature. If you alter our form by writing or typing in changes, be sure that you and all tenants initial the changes when you sign the document, so as to forestall any possibility that a tenant will claim you unilaterally inserted changes after he or she signed.

Again, as stressed in Clause 1, make sure all adults living in the rental unit, including both members of a married couple, sign the lease or rental agreement. And check that the tenant's name and signature match his or her driver's license or other legal document.

 Don't sign a lease until all terms are final and the tenant understands what's expected.
All of your expectations should be written into the lease or rental agreement (or any attachments, such as Rules and Regulations) before you and the tenant sign the document. Never sign an incomplete document assuming last-minute changes can be made later. And be sure your tenant clearly understands the lease or rental agreement before signing (this may mean you'll need to review it clause by clause). Chapter 4 discusses how to get your new tenancy off to the right start.

Give the tenant a copy of the signed lease or rental agreement.

 Help tenants understand the lease or rental agreement before they sign it.
Too many landlords thrust a lease or rental agreement at tenants and expect them to sign it unread. Far better to encourage tenants to ask questions about anything that's unclear, or actually review each clause with new tenants. It will save you lots of hassles later on.

If English is not a tenant's first language— especially if you regularly rent to people in the tenant's ethnic group—prepare and give the tenant a written translation. Some states require this. California, for example, requires landlords to notify Spanish-speaking tenants, in Spanish, of the right to request a Spanish version. But even if it's not legally required, you want your tenants to know and follow the rules. Providing a written translation of your lease or rental agreement is a great way to establish rapport with tenants.

 If you change the lease, have the cosigner sign the new version.
Generally speaking, a cosigner is bound only to the terms of the exact lease or rental agreement he cosigns. If you later change a significant term, add a new tenant or otherwise create a new contract, the original cosigner will probably be off the hook, unless you again get him to sign.

About Cosigners

Some landlords require cosigners on rental agreements and leases, especially when renting to students who depend on parents for much of their income. The cosigner signs a separate agreement or the rental agreement or lease, under which she agrees to cover any rent or damage-repair costs the tenant fails to pay.

In practice, a cosigner's promise to guarantee the tenant's rent obligation may have less legal value than at first you might think. This is because the threat of eviction is the primary factor that motivates a tenant to pay the rent, and obviously you cannot evict a cosigner. Also, since the cosigner must be sued separately in either a regular civil lawsuit or in small claims court, actually doing so—for example, if a tenant stiffs you for a month's rent—may be more trouble than it's worth. This is especially true if the cosigner lives in another state, since the amount of money you are out will rarely justify hiring a lawyer and collecting a judgment.

In sum, the benefits of having a lease or rental agreement cosigned by someone who won't be living on the property are largely psychological. But these benefits may still be worth something: A tenant who thinks you can (and will) notify and sue a cosigning relative or friend may be less likely to default on the rent. Similarly, a cosigner asked to pay the tenant's debts may persuade the tenant to pay.

If you decide to accept a cosigner, you may want to have that person fill out a separate rental application and agree to a credit check—after all, a cosigner who has no resources or connection to the tenant will be completely useless. Should the tenant and her prospective cosigner object to these inquiries and the costs of a credit check, you may wonder how serious they are about the guarantor's willingness to stand behind the tenant. Once you are satisfied that the cosigner can genuinely back up the tenant, add a line at the end of the lease or rental agreement for the dated signature, phone and address of the cosigner.

Month-to-Month Residential Rental Agreement

Clause 1. Identification of Landlord and Tenant

This Agreement is entered into between _____Marty Nelson_____ ("Tenant")
and _____Alex Stevens_____ ("Landlord"). Each Tenant is jointly
and severally liable for the payment of rent and performance of all other terms of this Agreement.

Clause 2. Identification of Premises

Subject to the terms and conditions in this Agreement, Landlord rents to Tenant, and Tenant
rents from Landlord, for residential purposes only, the premises located at _____
_____137 Howell St., Houston, Texas_____ ("the premises"),
together with the following furnishings and appliances: _____
_____.
Rental of the premises also includes _____
_____.

Clause 3. Limits on Use and Occupancy

The premises are to be used only as a private residence for Tenant(s) listed in Clause 1 of this
Agreement, and their minor children. Occupancy by guests for more than _ten days every six months_
is prohibited without Landlord's written consent and will be considered a breach of this Agreement.

Clause 4. Term of the Tenancy

The rental will begin on _____September 15_____, 199_X_, and continue on a
month-to-month basis. Landlord may terminate the tenancy or modify the terms of this Agreement by
giving the Tenant _____30_____ days written notice. Tenant may terminate the tenancy
by giving the Landlord _____30_____ days written notice.

Clause 5. Payment of Rent

Regular monthly rent.

Tenant will pay to Landlord a monthly rent of $_____900_____, payable in advance on the
first day of each month, except when that day falls on a weekend or legal holiday, in which case
rent is due on the next business day. Rent will be paid in the following manner, unless Landlord
designates otherwise:

Delivery of payment.

Rent will be paid:

[X] by mail, to _Alex Stevens (address below)_

[ ] in person, at _____

Form of payment.

Landlord will accept payment in these forms:

[X] personal check made payable to _Alex Stevens_

[X] cashier's check made payable to _Alex Stevens_

[ ] credit card

[X] money order

[ ] cash

Prorated first month's rent.

For the period from Tenant's move-in date, _September 15_, 199 _X_, through the end of the month, Tenant will pay to Landlord the prorated monthly rent of $ _450_. This amount will be paid on or before the date the Tenant moves in.

Clause 6. Late Charges

If Tenant fails to pay the rent in full before the end of the _third_ day after it's due, Tenant will pay Landlord a late charge as follows: _$10, plus $5 for each additional day that the rent remains unpaid. The total late charge for any one month will not exceed $45_. Landlord does not waive the right to insist on payment of the rent in full on the date it is due.

Clause 7. Returned Check and Other Bank Charges

If any check offered by Tenant to Landlord in payment of rent or any other amount due under this Agreement is returned for lack of sufficient funds, a "stop payment" or any other reason, Tenant will pay Landlord a returned check charge of $ _15_.

Clause 8. Deposit

On signing this Agreement, Tenant will pay to Landlord the sum of $ _1,800_ as a security deposit. Tenant may not, without Landlord's prior written consent, apply this security deposit to the last month's rent or to any other sum due under this Agreement. Within _30 days_ after Tenant has vacated the premises, returned keys and provided Landlord with a forwarding address, Landlord will return the deposit in full or give Tenant an itemized written statement of the reasons for, and the dollar amount of, any of the security deposit retained by Landlord, along with a check for any deposit balance.

[optional clauses here if any]

Clause 9. Utilities

Tenant will pay all utility charges, except for the following, which will be paid by Landlord: garbage and water _____

_____ .

Clause 10. Assignment and Subletting

Tenant will not sublet any part of the premises or assign this Agreement without the prior written consent of Landlord.

Clause 11. Tenant's Maintenance Responsibilities

Tenant will: (1) keep the premises clean, sanitary and in good condition and, upon termination of the tenancy, return the premises to Landlord in a condition identical to that which existed when Tenant took occupancy, except for ordinary wear and tear; (2) immediately notify Landlord of any defects or dangerous conditions in and about the premises of which Tenant becomes aware; and (3) reimburse Landlord, on demand by Landlord, for the cost of any repairs to the premises damaged by Tenant or Tenant's guests or business invitees through misuse or neglect.

Tenant has examined the premises, including appliances, fixtures, carpets, drapes and paint, and has found them to be in good, safe and clean condition and repair, except as noted in the Landlord/Tenant Checklist.

Clause 12. Repairs and Alterations by Tenant

a. Except as provided by law or as authorized by the prior written consent of Landlord, Tenant will not make any repairs or alterations to the premises, including nailing holes in the walls or painting the rental unit.

b. Tenant will not, without Landlord's prior written consent, alter, re-key or install any locks to the premises or install or alter any burglar alarm system. Tenant will provide Landlord with a key or keys capable of unlocking all such re-keyed or new locks as well as instructions on how to disarm any altered or new burglar alarm system.

Clause 13. Violating Laws and Causing Disturbances

Tenant is entitled to quiet enjoyment of the premises. Tenant and guests or invitees will not use the premises or adjacent areas in such a way as to: (1) violate any law or ordinance, including laws prohibiting the use, possession or sale of illegal drugs; (2) commit waste (severe property damage); or (3) create a nuisance by annoying, disturbing, inconveniencing or interfering with the quiet enjoyment and peace and quiet of any other tenant or nearby resident.

Clause 14. Pets

No animal, bird or other pet will be kept on the premises, even temporarily, except properly trained dogs needed by blind, deaf or disabled persons and _____ under the following conditions: _____ _____

_____ .

Clause 15. Landlord's Right to Access

Landlord or Landlord's agents may enter the premises in the event of an emergency, to make repairs or improvements or to show the premises to prospective buyers or tenants. Landlord may also enter the premises to conduct an annual inspection to check for safety or maintenance problems. Except in cases of emergency, Tenant's abandonment of the premises, court order, or where it is impractical to do so, Landlord shall give Tenant ___24 hours___ notice before entering.

Clause 16. Extended Absences by Tenant

Tenant will notify Landlord in advance if Tenant will be away from the premises for __seven__ or more consecutive days. During such absence, Landlord may enter the premises at times reasonably necessary to maintain the property and inspect for needed repairs.

Clause 17. Possession of the Premises

a. Tenant's failure to take possession.

If, after signing this Agreement, Tenant fails to take possession of the premises, Tenant will still be responsible for paying rent and complying with all other terms of this Agreement.

b. Landlord's failure to deliver possession.

If Landlord is unable to deliver possession of the premises to Tenant for any reason not within Landlord's control, including, but not limited to, partial or complete destruction of the premises, Tenant will have the right to terminate this Agreement upon proper notice as required by law. In such event, Landlord's liability to Tenant will be limited to the return of all sums previously paid by Tenant to Landlord.

Clause 18. Tenant Rules and Regulations

☒ Tenant acknowledges receipt of, and has read a copy of, tenant rules and regulations, which are attached to and incorporated into this Agreement by this reference.

Clause 19. Payment of Court Costs and Attorney Fees in a Lawsuit

In any action or legal proceeding to enforce any part of this Agreement, the prevailing party ☐ shall not / ☒ shall recover reasonable attorney fees and court costs.

Clause 20. Disclosures

Tenant acknowledges that Landlord has made the following disclosures regarding the premises:

☐   Disclosure of Information on Lead-Based Paint and/or Lead-Based Paint Hazards

☐   Other disclosures: _____

_____

_____

Clause 21. Authority to Receive Legal Papers

The Landlord, any person managing the premises and anyone designated by the Landlord are authorized to accept service of process and receive other notices and demands, which may be delivered to:

☒ The Landlord, at the following address: ___28 Franklin St., Houston, Texas, 77002___

_____

☐ The manager, at the following address: _____

_____

☐ The following person, at the following address: _____

_____

Clause 22. Additional Provisions

Additional provisions are as follows:

_____

_____

_____

_____

_____

_____

_____ .

Clause 23. Validity of Each Part

If any portion of this Agreement is held to be invalid, its invalidity will not affect the validity or enforceability of any other provision of this Agreement.

Clause 24. Grounds for Termination of Tenancy

The failure of Tenant or Tenant's guests or invitees to comply with any term of this Agreement is grounds for termination of the tenancy, with appropriate notice to Tenant and procedures as required by law.

Clause 25. Entire Agreement

This document constitutes the entire Agreement between the parties, and no promises or representations, other than those contained here and those implied by law, have been made by Landlord or Tenant. Any modifications to this Agreement must be in writing signed by Landlord and Tenant.

Sept. 1, 199X	_Alex Stevens_		Landlord
Date	Landlord or Landlord's Agent		Title

28 Franklin St.			
Street Address			

Houston, Texas 77002			713-555-1578
City, State & Zip			Phone

Sept. 1, 199X	_Marty Nelson_		713-555-8751
Date	Tenant		Phone

Date	Tenant		Phone

Date	Tenant		Phone

Disclosure of Information on Lead-Based Paint or Lead-Based Paint Hazards

Lead Warning Statement

Housing built before 1978 may contain lead-based paint. Lead from paint, paint chips and dust can pose health hazards if not managed properly. Lead exposure is especially harmful to young children and pregnant women. Before renting pre-1978 housing, lessors must disclose the presence of known lead-based paint and/or lead-based hazards in the dwelling. Lessees must also receive a federally approved pamphlet on lead poisoning prevention.

LESSOR'S DISCLOSURE

(a) Presence of lead-based paint and/or lead-based paint hazards. Check (i) or (ii) below:

☐ (i) Known lead-based paint and/or lead-based paint hazards are present in the housing (explain):_____.

☒ (ii) Lessor has no knowledge of lead-based paint and/or lead-based paint hazards in the housing.

(b) Records and reports available to the lessor. Check (i) or (ii) below:

☐ (i) Lessor has provided the lessee with all available records and reports pertaining to lead-based paint and/or lead-based paint hazards in the housing (list documents below):

_____.

☒ (ii) Lessor has no reports or records pertaining to lead-based paint or lead-based paint hazards in the housing.

LESSEE'S ACKNOWLEDGMENT (INITIAL)

_MN_ (c)   Lessee has received copies of all information listed above.

_MN_ (d)   Lessee has received the pamphlet Protect Your Family from Lead In Your Home.

AGENT'S ACKNOWLEDGMENT (INITIAL)

_____ (e)   Agent has informed the lessor of the lessor's obligations under 42 U.S.C 4852d and is aware of his/her responsibility to ensure compliance.

CERTIFICATION OF ACCURACY

The following parties have reviewed the information above and certify, to the best of their knowledge, that the information they have provided is true and accurate.

Alex Stevens	Sept. 1, 199X		
Lessor	Date	Lessor	Date
Marty Nelson	Sept. 1, 199X		
Lessee	Date	Lessee	Date
Agent	Date	Agent	Date

Choosing Tenants:
Your Most Important Decision

Choosing tenants is the most important decision any landlord makes. It should go almost without saying that to do it well and stay out of legal trouble, you need a good system. Follow the steps in this chapter to maximize your chances of selecting tenants who will pay their rent on time, keep their units in good condition and not cause you any legal or practical problems later.

 Before you advertise your property for rent, make a number of basic decisions—
including how much rent to charge, whether to offer a fixed-term lease or a month-to-month tenancy, how many tenants can occupy each rental unit, how big a security deposit to require and whether you'll allow pets. Making these important decisions should dovetail with writing your lease or rental agreement (see Chapter 2).

A. How to Advertise Rental Property

You can advertise rental property in many ways:
- putting an "Apartment for Rent" sign in front of the building or in one of the windows
- taking out classified newspaper ads
- posting flyers on neighborhood bulletin boards
- listing with a homefinders' or apartment-finding service that provides a centralized listing of rental units for a particular geographic area
- listing with a local real estate office that handles rentals
- buying ads in apartment rental guides or magazines
- hiring a management company that will advertise your rentals as part of the management fee, or
- posting a notice online, on a local electronic bulletin board or specialized newsgroup.

What will work best depends on a number of factors, including the characteristics of the particular rental property, its location, your budget and whether you are in a hurry to rent. Many smaller landlords find that instead of advertising widely and having to screen many potential tenants in an effort to sort the good from the bad, it makes better sense to market their rentals through word-of-mouth—telling friends, colleagues, neighbors and current tenants. After all, people who already live in your property will want decent neighbors.

But no matter how you let people know about the availability of your rental units, you want to follow these simple rules and stay out of legal hot water:

Describe the rental unit accurately. Your ad should be easy to understand and scrupulously honest. Also, as a practical matter, you should avoid abbreviations and real estate jargon in your ad. Include basic details, such as:
- rent
- size—particularly number of bedrooms and baths
- location—either the general neighborhood or street address
- lease or month-to-month rental agreement

- special features—such as fenced-in yard, view, washer/dryer, fireplace, remodeled kitchen, furnished, garage parking, doorman, hardwood floors or wall-to-wall carpeting
- phone number for more details (unless you're going to show the unit only at an open house and don't want to take calls), and
- date and time of any open house.

If you have any important rules (legal and nondiscriminatory, of course), such as no pets, put them in your ad. Letting prospective tenants know about your important policies can save you from talking to a lot of unsuitable people.

Be sure your ad can't be construed as discriminatory. The best way to do this is to focus only on the rental property—not on any particular type of tenant. Specifically, ads should never mention sex, race, religion, disability or age (unless yours is legally sanctioned senior citizens housing). And ads should never imply through words, photographs or illustrations that you prefer to rent to people because of their age, sex or race. (Section E, below, covers antidiscrimination laws.)

Quote an honest price in your ad. Or, put another way, if a tenant who is otherwise acceptable (has a good credit history, impeccable references and meets all the criteria laid out in Section D, below), shows up promptly and agrees to all the terms set out in your ad, he or she should be able to rent your property for the price you have advertised. By contrast, if you suddenly find a reason why it will cost

significantly more, you are likely to be in violation of your state's false advertising laws. This doesn't mean you are always legally required to rent at your advertised price, however. If a tenant asks for more services or significantly different lease terms that you feel require more rent, it's fine to bargain and raise your price, as long as your proposed increase doesn't violate any local rent control laws.

Don't advertise something you don't have. Some large landlords, management companies and rental services have advertised units that weren't really available in order to produce a large number of prospective tenants who could then be directed to higher-priced or inferior units. Such bait-and-switch advertising is clearly illegal under consumer fraud laws, and many property owners have been prosecuted for such practices.

Don't overhype security measures. Don't exaggerate your written or oral description of security measures. Not only will you have begun the landlord-tenant relationship on a note of insincerity, but your descriptions of security may legally obligate you to actually provide what you have portrayed. Or if you fail to do so, or fail to conscientiously maintain promised security measures in working order (such as outdoor lighting or an electronic gate on the parking garage), a court or jury may find your failure to be a material factor allowing a crime to occur on the premises. And if this happens, chances are good you will be held liable for a tenant's losses or injuries.

B. Renting Property That's Still Occupied

Often, you can wait until the old tenant moves out to show a rental unit to prospective tenants. This gives you the chance to refurbish the unit and avoids problems such as promising the place to a new tenant, only to have the existing tenant not move out on time or leave the place a mess.

To eliminate any gap in rent, however, you may want to show a rental unit while its current tenants are still there. This can create a conflict; in most states, you have a right to show the still-occupied property to prospective tenants, but your current tenants are still entitled to a reasonable level of privacy. (For details, see Clause 15, of the lease and rental agreement in Chapter 2.)

To minimize disturbing your current tenant, follow these guidelines:

- Before implementing your plans to find a new tenant, discuss them with outgoing tenants, so you can be as accommodating as possible.
- Give current tenants as much notice as possible before entering and showing a rental unit to prospective tenants.
- Try to limit the number of times you show the unit in a given week, and make sure your current tenants agree to any evening and weekend visits.
- Consider reducing the rent slightly for the existing tenant if showing the unit really will be an imposition.
- If possible, avoid putting a sign on the rental property itself, since this almost guarantees that your existing tenants will be bothered by strangers. Or, if you can't avoid putting up a sign, make sure any sign clearly warns against disturbing the occupant and includes a telephone number for information. Something on the order of "For Rent: Shown by Appointment Only. Call 555-1700. Do Not Disturb Occupants" should work fine.

If, despite your best efforts to protect their privacy, the current tenants are uncooperative or hostile, it really is best to avoid legal hassles and wait until they leave before showing the unit. Also, if the current tenant is a complete

slob or has damaged the place, you'll be far better off to apply paint and elbow grease before
trying to re-rent it.

C. Dealing With Prospective Tenants

It's good business, as well as a sound way to
protect yourself from future legal problems, to
carefully screen prospective tenants. To avoid
legal problems and choose the best tenant, ask
all prospective tenants to fill out a written
rental application that includes information on
the applicant's employment, income, credit
and rental housing history, including up-to-
date references. It's legal and a good idea to ask
for the applicant's Social Security and driver's
license numbers. You can also ask if the applicant has declared bankruptcy, been evicted or
been convicted of a crime. (You'll also get
much of this information from a credit report,
as discussed in Section D3, below.)

 *LeaseWriter includes a Rental Application
and a filled-in sample is shown below.*

Before giving prospective tenants a Rental
Application, complete the box at the top, filling
in the property address, the rental term and
any deposit or credit check fee that tenants
must pay before moving in. (Section D3, below, discusses credit check fees.)

Here are some basic guidelines for accept-
ing rental applications:

- Each prospective tenant—everyone age
18 or older who wants to live in your
rental property—should completely fill
out a separate written application. This
is true whether you're renting to a married couple or to unrelated roommates,
a complete stranger or the cousin of
your current tenant.
- Always make sure that prospective tenants complete the entire Rental Application, including Social Security number,
current employment, bank and emergency contacts. You may need this information later to track down a tenant who
skips town leaving unpaid rent or abandoned property.
- Ask each prospective tenant to show you
his driver's license or other photo identi-
fication as a way to verify that the applicant is using his real name.
- Be sure all potential tenants sign the
Rental Application, authorizing you to
verify the information and references.
(Some employers and banks require
written authorization before they will
talk to you.) You may also want to prepare a separate authorization, so that you
don't need to copy the entire application
and send it off every time a bank or employer wants proof that the tenant authorized you to verify the information.

 *LeaseWriter includes a Consent to Back-
ground and Reference Ckeck form and a
filled-in sample is shown below.*

Rental Application

SEPARATE APPLICATION REQUIRED FROM EACH APPLICANT AGE 18 OR OLDER.

THIS SECTION TO BE COMPLETED BY LANDLORD

Address of Property to Be Rented: _178 West 81st St., Apt. 4F_

Rental Term: ☐ month-to-month   ☒ lease from _March 1, 199X_ to _February 28, 199X_

Amounts Due Prior to Occupancy

First month's rent	$	1,500
Security deposit	$	1,500
Credit check fee	$	30
Other (specify): _Broker's fee_	$	1,500
TOTAL	$	4,530

Applicant

Full Name—include all names you use(d): _Hannah Silver_

Home Phone: (_609_) _555-3789_   Work Phone: (_609_) _555-4567_

Social Security Number: _123-00-4567_   Driver's License Number/State: _NJD123456_

Vehicle Make: _Toyota_   Model: _Tercel_   Color: _White_   Year: _1994_

License Plate Number/State: _NJ1234567_

Additional Occupants

List everyone, including children, who will live with you:

Full Name	Relationship to Applicant
Dennis Olson	Husband

Rental History

Current Address: _____39 Maple St., Princeton, NJ, 08540_____

Dates Lived at Address: _May 1990–date____ Reason for Leaving: _____New job in NY___

Landlord/Manager: _Jane Tucker_____ Landlord/Manager's Phone: (609) 555-7523

Previous Address: ____1215 Middlebrook Lane, Princeton, NJ, 08540_____

Dates Lived at Address: _June 1987-May 1990_ Reason for Leaving: _Better apartment___

Landlord/Manager: _Ed Palermo_____ Landlord/Manager's Phone: (609) 555-3711

Previous Address: ____1527 Highland Dr., New Brunswick, NJ, 08444_____

Dates Lived at Address: _Jan. 1986–June 1987_ Reason for Leaving: _to live closer to work_

Employment History

Name and Address of Current Employer: ____Argonworks, 54 Nassau St., Princeton, NJ__

_____ Phone:(609) 555-2333___

Name of Supervisor: ____Tom Schmidt_____ Supervisor's Phone:(609)555-2333___

Dates Employed at This Job: _____1983–date_____ Position or Title: _Marketing Director__

Name and Address of Previous Employer: ___Princeton Times_____

___13 Junction Rd., Princeton, NJ_____ Phone:(609) 555-1111____

Name of Supervisor: _Dory Krossber___ Supervisor's Phone:(609)555-2366_____

Dates Employed at This Job: __June 1982–Feb. 1983___ Position or Title: _Marketing Assistant_

Income

1. Your gross monthly employment income (before deductions): $ _5,000___

2. Average monthly amounts of other income (specify sources): $ _____
   Note: This does not include my husband's income. See his application.

_____

TOTAL: .... $ _____5,000_____

Credit and Financial Information

Bank/Financial Accounts	Account Number	Bank/Institution	Branch
Savings Account:	1222345	N.J. Federal	Trenton, N.J.
Checking Account:	789101	Princeton S&L	Princeton, N.J.
Money Market or Similar Account:	234789	City Bank	Princeton, N.J.

Credit Accounts & Loans	Type of Account (Auto loan, Visa, etc.)	Account Number	Name of Creditor	Amount Owed	Monthly Payment
Major Credit Card:	Visa	123456	City Bank	$1,000	$500
Major Credit Card:	Dept. Store	45789	Macy	$500	$500
Loan (mortgage, car,					
student loan, etc.):					
Other Major Obligations:					

Miscellaneous

Describe the number and type of pets you want to have in the rental property:

None now, but we might want to get a cat some time

Describe water-filled furniture you want to have in the rental property:

Do you smoke? ☐ yes   ☒ no

Have you ever: Filed for bankruptcy? ☐ yes   ☒ no   Been sued? ☐ yes   ☒ no

Been evicted? ☐ yes ☒ no   Been convicted of a crime? ☐ yes ☒ no

Explain any "yes" listed above:

References and Emergency Contact

Personal Reference: _Joan Stanley_   Relationship: _Friend, coworker_

Address: _785 Spruce St., Princeton, NJ, 08540_

_____ Phone: (_609_) 555-4578

Personal Reference: _Marnie Swatt_   Relationship: _Friend_

Address: _82 East 59th St., #12B, NYC_

_____ Phone: (_212_)555-8765

Contact in Emergency: _Connie & Martin Silver_   Relationship: _Parents_

Address: _7852 Pierce St., Somerset, NJ, 08321_

_____ Phone: (_609_) 555-7878

I certify that all the information given above is true and correct and understand that my lease or rental agreement may be terminated if I have made any false or incomplete statement in this application. I authorize verification of the information provided in this application from my credit sources, current and previous landlords and employers, and personal references.

February 15, 199X   _Hannah Silver_

Date   Applicant

Notes (Landlord/Manager): _____

_____

_____

_____

_____

_____

_____

D. Checking References, Credit History and More

If an application looks good, your next step is to follow up thoroughly. The time and money you spend are some of the most cost-effective expenditures you'll ever make.

⚠ Be consistent in your screening. *You risk a charge of illegal discrimination if you screen certain categories of applicants more stringently than others—for example, only requiring credit reports from racial minorities. Section E, below, discusses how to avoid illegal discrimination.*

Here are six steps of a very thorough screening process. You should always go through at least the first three to check out the applicant's previous landlords and income and employment, and run a credit check.

LeaseWriter includes a Tenant References Screening Form and a filled-in sample is shown below.

1. Check With Previous Landlords and Other References

Always call previous landlords or managers for references—even if you have a written letter of reference from a previous landlord. It's worth the cost of a long-distance phone call to weed out a tenant who may cause problems down the road. Also call employers and personal references listed on the application.

To organize the information you gather from these calls, use the Tenant References form, which lists key questions to ask previous landlords, employers and other references. Be sure to take notes of all your conversations and keep them on file. You may note your reasons

---

Consent to Background and Reference Check

I authorize ____Jan Gold_____ to obtain information about me from my credit sources, current and previous landlords and employers and personal references. I authorize my credit sources, current and previous landlords and employers and personal references to disclose to ____Jan Gold_____ such information about me as ____Jan Gold_____ may request.

Name ____Michael Clark_____

Address _____123 State Street, Chicago, Illinois_____

Phone Number _____312-555-9876_____

Date __February 2, 199X__   Applicant __Michael Clark_____

for refusing an individual on this form—for example, negative credit information, bad references from a previous landlord or your inability to verify information. You'll want a record of this information so that you can survive a fair housing challenge if a rejected applicant files a discrimination complaint against you. Also, as explained in Section F, below, you may have to divulge this information to a rejected applicant.

2. Verify Income and Employment

Obviously, you want to make sure that all tenants have the income to pay the rent each month. Call the prospective tenant's employer to verify income and length of employment. Make notes on the Tenant References form, discussed above.

Before providing this information, some employers require written authorization from the employee. You will need to mail or fax the employer a signed copy of the release included at the bottom of the Rental Application form or the separate Consent to Background and Reference Check form (Section C). If for any reason you question the income information you get by telephone—for example, you suspect a buddy of the applicant is exaggerating on his behalf—you may also ask applicants for copies of recent paycheck stubs.

It's also reasonable to require documentation of other sources of income, such as Social Security, disability payments, workers' compensation, welfare, child support or alimony.

How much income is enough? Think twice before renting to someone if the rent will take more than one-third of their income, especially if they have a lot of debts.

3. Obtain a Credit Report

Private credit reporting agencies collect and sell credit files and other information about tenants. Many landlords find it essential to check a prospective tenant's credit history with at least one credit reporting agency to see how responsible the person is about managing money.

a. How to Get a Credit Report

A credit report contains a gold mine of information on a prospective tenant. You can find out, for example, if a particular person has a history of paying rent or bills late, has gone through bankruptcy, been convicted of a crime or ever been evicted. (Your legal right to get information on evictions, however, may vary from state to state.) Credit reports usually cover the past seven to ten years. To run a credit check, you'll normally need a prospective tenant's name, address and Social Security number.

If you own many rental properties and need credit reports frequently, consider joining one of the three largest credit reporting agencies—Equifax, Trans Union or Experian (formerly TRW)—which charge about $20 to $30 in annual fees plus $10 to $15 per report. You can find their numbers and those of other tenant-

Tenant References

Name of Applicant: ___Michael Clark___

Address of Rental Unit: _123 State Street, Chicago, Illinois_

Previous Landlord or Manager

Contact (name, property owner or manager, address of rental unit):

___Kate Steiner, 345 Mercer St., Chicago, (312) 555-5432___

Date: ___February 4, 199x___

QUESTIONS

When did tenant rent from you (move-in and move-out dates)? ___December 1994 to date___

What was the monthly rent? ___$750___ Did tenant pay rent on time? _A week late a few times_

Was tenant considerate of neighbors—that is, no loud parties and fair, careful use of common areas? _Yes, considerate_

Did tenant have any pets? If so, were there any problems? _Yes, a cat, contrary to rental agreement_

Did tenant make any unreasonable demands or complaints? ___No___

Why did tenant leave? _He wants to live someplace that allows pets._

Did tenant give the proper amount of notice before leaving? ___Yes___

Did tenant leave the place in good condition? Did you need to use the security deposit to cover damage? ___No problems___

Any particular problems you'd like to mention? ___No___

Would you rent to this person again? ___Yes, but without pets___

Other Comments: _____

Employment Verification

Contact (name, company, position): _Brett Field, Manager, Chicago Car Company_

Date: _February 5, 199X_ Salary: _$30,000_ Dates of Employment: _March 1993 to date_

Comments: _No problems. Fine employee. Michael is responsible and hard-working._

Personal Reference

Contact (name and relationship to applicant): _Sandy Cameron, friend_

Date: _February 5, 199X_ How long have you known the applicant? _Five years_

Would you recommend this person as a prospective tenant? _Yes_

Comments: _Michael is very neat and responsible. He's reliable and will be a great tenant._

Credit and Financial Information

Mostly fine—see attached credit report

Notes (including reasons for rejecting applicant)

Applicant had a history of late rent payments.

screening companies in the Yellow Pages under "Credit Reporting Agencies." Your state or local apartment association may also offer credit reporting services. With some credit reporting agencies, you can obtain an oral credit report the same day it's requested, and a written one within a day or two.

b. Credit Check Fees

It's legal in most states to charge prospective tenants a fee for the cost of the credit report itself and your time and trouble. Any credit check fee should be reasonably related to the cost of the credit check—$20 to $30 is common.

Many landlords don't charge credit check fees, preferring to absorb the cost as they would any other cost of business. For low-end units, charging an extra fee can be a barrier to getting tenants in the first place, and a tenant who pays a fee but is later rejected is likely to be annoyed and possibly more apt to claim that you have rejected her for a discriminatory reason.

The Rental Application form in this book informs prospective tenants if you charge a credit check fee. Be sure prospective tenants understand that paying a credit check fee does not guarantee the tenant will get the rental unit.

 It's a mistake to collect a credit check fee from lots of people. *If you expect a large number of applicants, you'd be wise not to accept fees from everyone. Instead, read over the applications first and do a credit check only on applicants you're seriously considering. That way, you won't waste your time (and prospective tenants' money) collecting fees from unqualified applicants.*

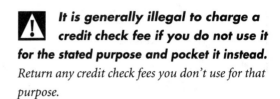 **It is generally illegal to charge a credit check fee if you do not use it for the stated purpose and pocket it instead.** *Return any credit check fees you don't use for that purpose.*

c. What You're Looking For in a Credit Report

As you surely know, it makes sense to be leery of applicants with lots of debts—this clearly includes people whose monthly payments plus the rent obligation exceed 40% of their after-tax income. Also, look at the person's bill-paying habits, and of course pay attention to lawsuits and evictions.

Sometimes, your only choice is to rent to someone with poor or fair credit—or even no credit (for example, a student or recent graduate). If that's your situation, you should still adopt sensible screening requirements such as these:

• positive references from previous landlords and employers
• a creditworthy cosigner of the lease (see the discussion on cosigners at the end of Chapter 2)
• a good-sized deposit—as much as you can collect under state law and the market will bear (see Clause 8 of the form agreements in Chapter 2), and
• proof of specific steps taken to improve bad credit—for example, enrolling in a debt-counseling group.

4. Verify Bank Account Information

If an individual's credit history raises questions about financial stability, you may want to double-check the bank accounts listed on the rental application. If so, you'll probably need an authorization form such as the one included at the bottom of the Rental Application, or the separate Consent to Background and Reference Check form (discussed in Section C, above). Banks differ as to the type of information they will provide over the phone. Generally, without a written authorization, banks will only confirm that an individual has an account there and that it is in good standing.

 Be wary of an applicant who has no checking or savings account. *Tenants who offer to pay cash or with a money order should be viewed with extreme caution. Perhaps the individual bounced so many checks that the bank dropped the account or the income comes from a shady or illegitimate source—for example, from drug dealing.*

5. Review Court Records

If your prospective tenant has previously lived in your area, you may want to review local court records to see if collection or eviction lawsuits have ever been filed against him. Checking court records may seem like overkill, since some of this information may be available on credit reports, but now and then it's an in-

valuable tool if you are able to weed out a prospective tenant who is almost sure to be a troublemaker. Especially if you fear that the person who rubs you the wrong way might accuse you of illegal discrimination if you turn down her application, you'll want to have good documentation of your decision. Because court records are kept for many years, this kind of information can supplement references from recent landlords. Talk to the court clerk at the local court that handles eviction cases for information on how to check court records.

E. Avoiding Illegal Discrimination

Federal and state antidiscrimination laws limit what you can say and do in the tenant selection process. Basically, you need to keep in mind three important points:

1. You are legally free to choose among prospective tenants as long as your decisions are based on legitimate business criteria. You are entitled to reject people for the following reasons:
- poor credit history
- income that you reasonably regard as insufficient to pay the rent
- negative references from previous landlords indicating problems—such as property damage or consistently late rent payments—that make someone a bad risk

- convictions for criminal offenses
- inability to meet the legal terms of a lease or rental agreement, such as someone who can't come up with the security deposit or who wants to keep a pet and your policy is no pets, or
- more people than you want to live in the unit—assuming that your limit on the number of tenants is clearly tied to health and safety or legitimate business needs. (See Clause 3 discussion of occupancy limits in Chapter 2.)

2. Antidiscrimination laws specify clearly illegal reasons to refuse to rent to a tenant. The federal Fair Housing Act (42 U.S. Code §§ 3601-3619) prohibits discrimination on the basis of race or color, religion, national origin, gender, age, familial status (children) and physical or mental disability (including recovering alcoholics and people with a past drug addiction). Many states and cities also prohibit discrimination based on marital status or sexual orientation.

For more information on the rules and regulations of the Fair Housing Act, contact HUD's Fair Housing Information Clearinghouse at 800-343-3442.

For information on state and local housing discrimination laws, contact your state fair housing agency.

3. Consistency is crucial when dealing with prospective tenants. If you don't treat all tenants more or less equally—for example, if you arbitrarily set tougher standards (such as a higher income level or proof of legal status, such as legal papers) for renting to a member of an ethnic minority—you are violating federal laws and opening yourself up to expensive lawsuits and the possibility of being hit with large judgments. On the other hand, if you require *all* prospective tenants to meet the same income standard and to supply satisfactory proof of their legal eligibility to work (as well as meet your other criteria), you will get the needed information but in a nondiscriminatory way.

Show the property to and accept applications from everyone who's interested.

Even if, after talking to someone on the phone, you doubt that a particular tenant can qualify, it's best to politely take all applications. Unless you can point to something in writing that clearly disqualifies a tenant, you are always on shaky legal ground. Refusing to take an application may unnecessarily anger a prospective tenant, and may make him or her more likely to look into the possibility of filing a discrimination complaint. Make decisions later about who will rent the property. Be sure to keep copies of all applications. (See discussion of recordkeeping in Chapter 4, Section D.)

The Rights of Disabled Tenants

The Fair Housing Act requires that landlords *accommodate* the needs of disabled tenants, at the landlord's own expense. (42 U.S. Code § 3604 (f) (B) (1988).) You are expected to adjust your rules, procedures or services in order to give a person with a disability an equal opportunity to use and enjoy a dwelling unit or a common space. Accommodations include such things as providing a close-in, spacious parking space for a wheelchair-bound tenant. Your duty to accommodate disabled tenants does not mean that you must bend every rule and change every procedure at the tenant's request. You are expected to accommodate "reasonable" requests, but need not undertake changes that would seriously impair your ability to run your business.

The Fair Housing Act also requires landlords to allow disabled tenants to make reasonable modifications of their living unit at their expense if that is what is needed for the person to comfortably and safely live in the unit. (42 U.S. Code § 3604 (f) (3) (A) (1988).) For example, a disabled person has the right to modify his living space to the extent necessary to make the space safe and comfortable, as long as the modifications will not make the unit unacceptable to the next tenant or the disabled tenant agrees to undo the modification when he leaves. Examples of modifications undertaken by a disabled tenant include lowering countertops for a wheelchair-bound tenant.

You are not obliged to allow a disabled tenant to modify his unit at will, without your prior approval. You are entitled to ask for a reasonable description of the proposed modifications, proof that they will be done in a workmanlike manner and evidence that the tenant is obtaining any necessary building permits. Moreover, if a tenant proposes to modify the unit in such a manner that will require restoration when the tenant leaves (such as the repositioning of lowered kitchen counters), you may require that the tenant pay into an interest-bearing escrow account the amount estimated for the restoration. (The interest belongs to the tenant.)

F. Choosing—and Rejecting—an Applicant

After you've collected applications and done some screening, you can start sifting through the applicants. Section D, above, covers the basic criteria you need to evaluate when choosing tenants. Start by eliminating the worst risks—people with negative references from previous landlords, a history of nonpayment of rent or poor credit or previous evictions. Then make your selection.

Assuming you choose the best-qualified candidate (based on income, credit history and references), you have no legal problem. But what if you have a number of more or less equally qualified applicants? Can you safely choose an older white man over a young black woman? The answer is a qualified "yes." If two people rate equally, you can legally choose either one without legal risk in any particular situation. But be extra careful not to take the further step of always selecting a person of the same sex, age or ethnicity. For example, if you are a larger landlord who is frequently faced with tough choices and who always avoids an equally qualified minority or disabled applicant, you are guilty of discrimination.

1. Recordkeeping

A crucial use of any tenant-screening system is to document how and why you chose a particular tenant.

Be sure to note your reasons for rejection—such as poor credit history, pets (if you don't accept pets) or a negative reference from a previous landlord—on the Tenant References form or other document so that you have a paper trail if a tenant ever accuses you of illegal discrimination. You want to be able to back up your reason for rejecting the person. Keep organized files of applications, credit reports and other materials and notes on prospective tenants for at least three years after you rent a particular unit. (See the discussion of recordkeeping in Chapter 4, Section D.)

2. Information You Must Provide Rejected Applicants

If you reject an applicant based on information from a third party, such as a credit report,

former landlord, employer or bank, the federal Fair Credit Reporting Act requires you to give this information to the applicant upon request. (15 U.S.C. §§ 1681 et. seq.) The federal requirements do not apply if you reject someone based on information in his application alone or information received after you interview the applicant.

Exactly what you must disclose, and how to do it, depends on the basis for your rejection—for example, different rules apply to information you receive from a previous landlord versus a credit-reporting agency.

Credit reports. If you do not rent to someone (or you charge a higher rent) because of negative information in his credit report or an insufficient credit report, you must give the applicant the name and address of the agency that provided the credit report. You must tell the applicant that he or she has a right to obtain a copy of the file from the agency that reported the negative information, by requesting it within the next 60 days. You must also tell the rejected applicant that the credit reporting agency did not make the decision to reject him as a tenant and cannot explain the reason for the rejection. Finally, you must tell applicants that they can dispute the accuracy of their credit report and add their own consumer statement to their report.

Landlords, employers and other sources of information. If you reject an applicant based on negative information from a previous landlord, employer, personal reference, bank, court clerk or court record or store, you must advise the applicant of his rights at the time you reject him. Specifically, you must tell rejected applicants that they have a right to send you a written request for disclosure of the negative information from the third party (other than a credit reporting agency) within the next 60 days. If a disappointed applicant sends you a request, you must disclose within a reasonable time "the nature of the information" that led to your decision.

Unfortunately, the Fair Credit Reporting Act itself does not specify how much information you must divulge. We suggest you use the most general approach possible ("I received negative information from your personal reference John Smith"), rather than come clean with the dirty details ("John Smith told me you were a complete slob, were frequently overdrawn on your checking account and had a lot of strange friends.")

G. Choosing a Tenant-Manager

Many landlords hire a manager to handle all the day-to-day details of running a rental property, including fielding tenants' routine repair requests and collecting the rent. If you hire a resident manager, make sure he or she (like all other tenants) completes a rental application and that you check references and other information carefully. If you use a property management company, it will do this work for you. (See Section H, below.)

The person you hire as a manager will occupy a critical position in your business. Your manager will interact with every tenant and will often have access to her personal files and her home. Legally, you have a duty to protect your tenants from injuries caused by employees you know (or should know) pose a risk of harm to others. If someone gets hurt or has property stolen or damaged by a manager whose background you didn't check carefully, you could be sued, so it's crucial that you be especially vigilant when hiring a manager.

When you hire a manager, you should sign two separate agreements:

- An employer agreement that covers manager responsibilities, hours and pay that can be terminated at any time for any reason by either party.
- A month-to-month rental agreement that can be terminated by either of you with the amount of notice, typically 30 days, required under state law.

Whether or not you compensate a manager with reduced rent or regular salary, be sure you comply with your legal obligations as an employer, such as following laws governing minimum wage and overtime.

Every Landlord's Legal Guide *by Marcia Stewart, Ralph Warner and Janet Portman (Nolo Press), provides detailed advice on hiring a manager, including how to prepare a property manager agreement.*

The Employer's Legal Handbook, *by Fred S. Steingold (Nolo Press), is a complete guide to the latest workplace laws and regulations. It covers everything you need to know about hiring and firing employees, personnel policies, employee benefits, discrimination and other laws affecting small business practices.*

H. Property Management Companies

Property management companies are often used by owners of large apartment complexes and by absentee owners too far away from the property to be directly involved in everyday details. Property management companies generally take care of renting units, collecting rent, taking tenant complaints, arranging repairs and maintenance and evicting troublesome tenants. Of course, some of these responsibilities may be shared with or delegated to resident managers who, in some instances, may work for the management company.

A variety of relationships between owners and management companies are possible, depending on your wishes and how the particular management company chooses to do business. For example, if you own one or more big buildings, the management company will probably recommend hiring a resident manager. But if your rental property has only a few units, or you own a number of small buildings spread over a good-sized geographical area, the management company will probably suggest simply responding to tenant requests and complaints from its central office.

One advantage of working with a management company is that you avoid all the legal hassles of being an employer: paying payroll taxes, buying workers' compensation insurance, withholding income tax. The management company is an independent contractor, not an employee. It hires and pays the people who do the work. Typically, you sign a contract spelling out the management company's duties and fees. Most companies charge a fixed percentage—about 5% to 10%—of the total rent collected. (The salary of any resident manager is additional.) This gives the company a good incentive to keep the building filled with rent-paying tenants.

Another advantage is that management companies are usually well informed about the law, keep good records and are adept at staying out of legal hot water in such areas as discrimination, invasion of privacy and returning deposits.

The primary disadvantage of hiring a management company is the expense. For example, if you pay a management company 10% of the $14,000 you collect in rent each month from tenants in a 20-unit building, this amounts to $1,400 a month and $16,800 per year. While many companies charge less than 10%, it's still quite an expense. Also, if the management company works from a central office with no one on-site, tenants may feel that management is too distant and unconcerned with their day-to-day needs.

Management companies have their own contracts, which you should read thoroughly and understand before signing. Be sure you understand how the company is paid and its exact responsibilities.

■

Getting the Tenant Moved In

Legal disputes between landlords and tenants have gained a reputation for being almost as emotional as divorce court battles. While some may be inevitable, we believe many disputes could be diffused at the start if tenants were better educated as to their legal rights and responsibilities. A clearly written and easy-to-understand lease or rental agreement that details a tenant's obligations and is signed by all adult occupants of your rental unit is the key to starting a tenancy. (See Chapter 2.) But we believe there's more that can be done to help establish a positive relationship when new tenants move in. Most importantly, you should:

- Inspect the property, fill out a Landlord/Tenant Checklist with the tenant and photograph the rental unit.
- Prepare a move-in letter highlighting important terms of the tenancy and your expectations.

A. Inspect and Photograph the Unit

To eliminate the possibility of all sorts of future arguments, it is absolutely essential that you (or your representative) and prospective tenants (together, if possible) check the place over for damage and obvious wear and tear before the tenant moves in. The best way to document what you find is to jointly fill out a Landlord/Tenant Checklist form and take photographs of the rental unit.

1. Fill Out the Landlord/Tenant Checklist

A Landlord/Tenant Checklist, inventorying the condition of the rental property at the beginning and end of the tenancy, is an excellent device to protect both you and your tenant when the tenant moves out and wants the security deposit returned. Without some record as to the condition of the unit, the tenant is all too likely to make unreasonable demands. For example, is there a landlord alive who has not been falsely told that stains in the rug or a cracked mirror or broken stove were already damaged when the tenant moved in?

The checklist provides good evidence as to why you withheld all or part of a security deposit. And coupled with a system to regularly keep track of the rental property's condition, the checklist will also be extremely useful to you if a tenant withholds rent, breaks the lease and moves out or sues you outright, claiming the unit needs substantial repairs.

 LeaseWriter includes a Landlord/Tenant Checklist and a filled-in sample is shown below.

Landlord/Tenant Checklist

GENERAL CONDITION OF ROOMS

572 Fourth St.   Apt. 11   Washington, D.C.

Street Address   Unit Number   City

	Condition on Arrival	Condition on Departure	Estimated Cost of Repair/Replacement
LIVING ROOM			
Floors & Floor Coverings	OK		
Drapes & Window Coverings	Mini-blinds discolored		
Walls & Ceilings	OK		
Light Fixtures	OK		
Windows, Screens & Doors	Window rattles		
Front Door & Locks	OK		
Fireplace	N/A		
Other			
Other			
KITCHEN			
Floors & Floor Coverings	Cigarette burn hole		
Walls & Ceilings	OK		
Light Fixtures	OK		
Cabinets	OK		
Counters	Stained		
Stove/Oven	Burners filthy (grease)		
Refrigerator	OK		
Dishwasher	OK		
Garbage Disposal	N/A		
Sink & Plumbing	OK		
Windows, Screens & Doors	OK		
Other			
Other			
DINING ROOM			
Floors & Floor Covering	OK		
Walls & Ceiling	Crack in ceiling		
Light Fixtures	OK		
Windows, Screens & Doors	OK		

	Condition on Arrival	Condition on Departure	Estimated Cost of Repair/Replacement
Other			
Other			
BATHROOM(S)	**Bath 1 Bath 2**	**Bath 1 Bath 2**	
Floors & Floor Coverings	OK		
Walls & Ceilings	OK		
Windows, Screens & Doors	OK		
Light Fixtures	OK		
Bathtub/Shower	Tub chipped		
Sink & Counters	OK		
Toilet	Base of toilet dirty		
Other			
Other			
BEDROOM(S)	**Bdrm 1 Bdrm 2 Bdrm 3**	**Bdrm 1 Bdrm 2 Bdrm 3**	
Floors & Floor Coverings			
Windows, Screens & Doors	OK OK		
Walls & Ceilings	OK OK		
Light Fixtures	Dented OK		
Other	Mildew in closet		
Other			
OTHER AREAS			
Heating System	OK		
Air Conditioning	OK		
Lawn/Garden	OK		
Stairs & Hallway	N/A		
Patio, Terrace Deck, etc.	N/A		
Basement	OK		
Parking Area	OK		
Other			
Other			

☒ Tenants acknowledge that all smoke detectors and fire extinguishers were tested in their presence and found to be in working order, and that the testing procedure was explained to them. Tenants agree to test all detectors at least once a month and to report any problems to Landlord/Manager in writing. Tenants agree to replace all smoke detector batteries as necessary.

FURNISHED PROPERTY

	Condition on Arrival	Condition on Departure	Estimated Cost of Repair/Replacement
LIVING ROOM			
Coffee Table	Two scratches on top		
End Tables	OK		
Lamps	OK		
Chairs	OK		
Sofa	OK		
Other			
Other			
KITCHEN			
Broiler Pan	N/A		
Ice Trays	N/A		
Other			
Other			
DINING AREA			
Chairs	OK		
Stools	N/A		
Table	Leg bent slightly		
Other			
BATHROOM(S)	Bath 1 Bath 2	Bath 1 Bath 2	
Mirrors			
Shower Curtain	OK		
Hamper	Torn		
Other	N/A		
BEDROOM(S)	Bdrm 1 Bdrm 2 Bdrm 3	Bdrm 1 Bdrm 2 Bdrm 3	
Beds (single)	OK N/A		
Beds (double)	N/A OK		
Chairs	OK OK		
Chests	NA N/A		
Dressing Tables	OK N/A		
Lamps	OK OK		
Mirrors	OK OK		
Night Tables	OK N/A		
Other			

	Condition on Arrival	Estimated Cost of Condition on Departure	Repair/Replacement
Other			
OTHER AREAS			
Bookcases	N/A		
Desks	N/A		
Pictures	Hallway picture frame chipped		
Other			
Other			

Use this space to provide any additional explanation:

_____

_____

_____

_____

_____

_____

_____

_____

_____

Landlord/Tenant Checklist completed on moving in on ___May 1_____, 199 _X_, and approved by:

____*Bernard Cohen*_____ and _____*Maria Crouse*_____

Landlord/Manager   Tenant

                                                    Sandra Martino
                                    _____

                                                    Tenant

                                    _____

                                                    Tenant

Landlord/Tenant Checklist completed on moving out on _____, 199____, and approved by:

_____ and _____

Landlord/Manager   Tenant

                                    _____

                                                    Tenant

                                    _____

                                                    Tenant

Several states require landlords to give new tenants a written statement on the condition of the rental premises at move-in time, including a comprehensive list of existing damages. See the 50-State Law Browser for details.

You and the tenant should fill out the checklist together. If that's impossible, complete the form and then make a copy and give it to the tenant to review. You should ask the tenant to note any disagreement promptly and return the checklist to you.

The checklist is in two parts. The first side covers the general condition of each room. The second side covers furnishings, such as a living room lamp or bathroom shower curtain. Obviously, you can simply mark "Not Applicable" or "N/A" in most of these boxes if your unit is not furnished or does not have a particular item listed.

If your rental property has rooms or furnishings not listed on the form, note them in "Other Areas" or cross out something that you don't have and write in the changes. If you are renting out a large house or apartment or providing many furnishings, you may want to attach a separate sheet.

In the *Condition on Arrival* column, mark "OK" in the space next to items that are in satisfactory condition. Make a note—as specific as possible—on items that are not working or are dirty, worn, scratched or simply not in the best condition. For example, don't simply note that the refrigerator "needs fixing" if an ice maker doesn't work—it's just as easy to write "ice maker broken, should not be used." This way, if the tenant uses the ice maker anyway and causes water damage in the unit below, he cannot claim that you failed to tell him.

The last two columns—*Condition on Departure* and *Estimated Cost of Repair or Replacement*—are for use when the tenant moves out and, ideally, the two of you inspect the unit again. At that time the checklist will document your need to make deductions from the security deposit for repairs or cleaning or to replace missing items. (Chapter 5, Section D, discusses returning security deposits.) If you don't know what it will cost to fix or replace something, simply write in "Cost will be documented by Landlord."

As part of your move-in procedures, make sure you test all smoke detectors and fire extinguishers in the tenant's presence and show them to be in good working order. Clearly explain to the tenant how to test the smoke detectors and point out the signs—for example, a beeping noise—of a failing detector. Alert tenants to their responsibility to regularly test smoke detectors, and explain how to replace the battery when necessary. Be sure the tenant checks the box on the bottom of the first page of the checklist acknowledging that the smoke detector was tested in his presence and shown to be in working order. By doing this, you'll limit your liability if the smoke detector fails and results in fire damage or injury.

After you and the tenant agree on all of the particulars on the rental unit, you each should sign and date the checklist, as well as any attachments, on both sides. Keep the original for yourself and attach a copy to the tenant's lease or rental agreement. (See Clause 11 of the form agreements in Chapter 2.)

Be sure to keep the checklist up-to-date if you repair, replace, add or remove items or furnishings after the tenant moves in. Both you and the tenant should initial and date any changes.

2.   Photograph the Rental Unit

Taking photos or videotapes of the unit before the tenant moves in is another excellent way to avoid disputes over a tenant's responsibility for damage and dirt. In addition to the checklist, you'll be able to compare "before" and "after" pictures when a tenant leaves. This should help refresh your tenant's memory and may result in her being more reasonable. Certainly, if you end up in mediation or court for not returning the full security deposit, being able to document your point of view with photos will be invaluable. In addition, photos or a video can also help if you have to sue a former tenant for cleaning and repair costs above the deposit amount.

It's best to take "before" photographs with a Polaroid camera that develops pictures on the spot. This will allow both you and the tenant to date and sign the pictures, each keeping a set. Otherwise, use a camera that automatically imprints the date on each photo.

If you make a video, get the tenant on tape saying the date and time so that you can prove when the video was made, and later provide him with a copy.

If possible, you should repeat this process after the tenant leaves, as part of your standard move-out procedure. (Chapter 5, Section B, discusses how to prepare a move-out letter.)

B.   Send New Tenants a Move-In Letter

A move-in letter should dovetail with the lease or rental agreement and provide basic information, such as the manager's phone number and office hours.

You can also use a move-in letter to explain any procedures and rules that are too detailed or numerous to include in your lease or rental agreement. (Alternatively, large landlords may use a set of Rules and Regulations to cover some of these issues. See Clause 18 of the form agreements in Chapter 2.)

Here are some items you may want to cover in a move-in letter:

- any lock-out or re-key fees
- use of grounds and garage
- your policy regarding rent increases for additional roommates
- location of garbage cans, available recycling programs and trash pickup days
- maintenance do's and don'ts, such as how to avoid overloading circuits and use the garbage disposal properly
- renter's insurance
- other issues, such as pool hours, elevator operation, building access during evening hours and use of a laundry room and storage space, should be covered as needed.

Move-In Letter

September 1, 199X
_____
Date
Frank O'Hara
_____
Tenant
139 Porter Street
_____
Street address
Madison, Wisconsin 53704
_____
City and State

Dear_____Frank_____,
                    Tenant

Welcome to _____ Apartment 45 B at Happy Hill Apartments _____
_____ (address of rental unit). We hope you will enjoy living here. This letter
is to explain what you can expect from the management and what we'll be looking for from you:

1. **Rent:** There is no grace period for the payment of rent. (See Clauses 5 and 6 of your rental
   agreement for details, including late charges.) Also, we don't accept post-dated checks. .

2. **New roommates:** If you want someone to move in as a roommate, please contact us first.
   If your rental unit is big enough to accommodate another person, we will arrange for the new person
   to fill out a rental application. If it's approved, all of you will need to sign a new rental agreement.
   Depending on the situation, there may be a rent increase to add a roommate. .

3. **Notice to end tenancy:** To terminate your month-to-month tenancy, you must give at least 30 days'
   written notice. We have a written form available for this purpose. We may also terminate the tenancy,
   or change its terms, on 30 days' written notice. If you give less than 30 days' notice, you will still be
   financially responsible for rent for the balance of the 30-day period.

4. **Deposits:** Your security deposit will be applied to costs of cleaning, damages or unpaid rent after you
   move out. You may not apply any part of the deposit toward any part of your rent in the last month of
   your tenancy. (See Clause 8 of your rental agreement.) .

5. **Manager:** Sophie Beauchamp (Apartment #15, phone 555-1234) is your resident manager. You should
   pay your rent to her and promptly let her know of any maintenance or repair problems (see #7, below) and
   any other questions or problems. She's in her office every day from 8 a.m. to 10 a.m. and from 4 p.m. to
   6 p.m. and can be reached by phone at other times.

6. **Landlord-Tenant Checklist:** By now, Sophie Beauchamp should have taken you on a walk-through of
   your apartment to check the condition of all walls, drapes, carpets and appliances and to test the
   smoke alarms and fire extinguisher. These are all listed on the Landlord-Tenant Checklist, which you
   should have reviewed carefully and signed. When you move out, we will ask you to check each item
   against its original condition as described on the Checklist. .

7. Maintenance/Repair Problems: We are determined to maintain a clean, safe building in which all systems are in good repair. To help us make repairs promptly, we will give you Maintenance/Repair Request forms to report to the manager any problems in your apartment, such as a broken garbage disposal, or on the building or grounds, such a burned-out light in the garage. (Extra copies are available from the manager.) In an emergency, or when it's not convenient to use this form, please call the manager at 555-1234.

8. Semi-Annual Safety and Maintenance Update: To help us keep your unit and the common areas in excellent condition, we'll ask you to fill out a form every six months updating any problems on the premises or in your rental unit. This will allow you to report any potential safety hazards or other problems that otherwise might be overlooked.

9. Annual Safety Inspection: Once a year, we will ask to inspect the condition and furnishings of your rental unit and update the Landlord-Tenant Checklist. In keeping with state law, we will give you reasonable notice before the inspection, and you are encouraged to be present for it.

10. Insurance: We highly recommend that you purchase renters' insurance. The building property insurance policy will not cover the replacement of your personal belongings if they are lost due to fire, theft or accident. In addition, you could be found liable if someone is injured on the premises you rent as a result of your negligence. If you damage the building itself—for example, if you start a fire in the kitchen and it spreads—you could be responsible for large repair bills.

11. Moving Out: It's a little early to bring up moving out, but please be aware that we have a list of items that should be cleaned before we conduct a move-out inspection. If you decide to move, please ask the manager for a copy of our Move-Out Letter, explaining our procedures for inspection and returning your deposit.

12. Telephone Number Changes: Please notify us if your home or work phone number changes, so we can reach you promptly in an emergency.

Please let us know if you have any questions.

Sincerely,

September 1, 199X   *Tom Guiliano*
Date   Owner

I have read and received a copy of this statement.

September 1, 199X   *Frank O'Hara*
Date   Tenant

Resident's Maintenance/Repair Request

Date: _____ August 29, 199X _____

Address: _____ 392 Main St., #402, Houston, Texas _____

Resident's Name: _____ Mary Griffin _____

Phone (home): _____ 555-4321 _____ Phone (work): _____ 555-5679 _____

Problem (be as specific as possible): _____ Garbage disposal doesn't work _____

Best time to make repairs: _____ After 6 p.m. or Saturday morning _____

Other comments: _____

I authorize entry into my unit to perform the maintenance or repair requested above, in my absence, unless stated otherwise above.

Mary Griffin
_____
Resident

. . . .
FOR MANAGEMENT USE

Work done: _____ Fixed garbage disposal (removed spoon) _____

Time spent: _____ 1/2 _____ hours

Date completed: _____ August 30 _____, 199 X

Unable to complete on _____, 199____, because: _____

Notes and comments: _____

August 30, 199X _____ _Hal Ortiz_ _____
_____
Date _____ Landlord/Manager

Time Estimate for Repair

Stately Manor Apartments
_____

August 30, 199X
_____
Date

Mary Griffin
_____
Tenant

392 Main St., #402
_____
Street address

Houston, Texas
_____
City and State

Dear____Mary Griffin_____,

            Tenant

Thank you for promptly notifying us of the following problem with your unit:

Garbage disposal doesn't work
_____
_____
_____
_____
_____
_____

We expect to have the problem corrected on _____September 3_____, 199__X__, due to

the following:

Garbage disposal part is out of stock locally, but has been ordered and will be

delivered in a day or two.
_____
_____
_____

We regret any inconvenience this delay may cause. Please do not hesitate to point out any other

problems that may arise.

Sincerely,

Hal Ortiz
_____
Landlord/Manager

Notice of Intent to Enter Dwelling Unit

To: ___Anna Rivera_____
Tenant
   123 East Avenue, Apt. #4
_____
Street address
   Rochester, New York
_____
City and State

THIS NOTICE is to inform you that on _____January 7, 199X_____,

[X] at approximately ____1:00____ AM/PM the landlord, or the landlord's agent, will enter the

premises for the following reason:

[X] To make or arrange for the following repairs or improvements:

   _fix garbage disposal_____

_____

_____

_____

_____

[ ] To show the premises to:

   [ ] a prospective tenant or purchaser

   [X] workers or contractors regarding the above repair or improvement

[ ] Other: _____

_____

_____

You are, of course, welcome to be present. If you have any questions or if the date or time is

inconvenient, please notify me promptly at _____716-555-7899_____.

                                         Phone number

_January 5, 199X_____   _Marlene Morgan_____
Date   Landlord/Manager

A move-in letter is a good place to explain how and where tenants should report maintenance and repair problems.

LeaseWriter *includes a Resident's Main tenance/Repair Request form for tenants to use to request specific repairs, and a Time Estimate for Repair form to let tenants know when repairs will be made.*
LeaseWriter *also includes a Notice of Intent to Enter Dwelling Unit form to notify the tenant when you will be entering the rental property for legally allowed reasons such as to make repairs. Filled-in samples of all three forms are shown above.*

Because every rental situation is at least a little different, we cannot supply you with a generic move-in letter that will work for everyone. You can use the sample shown here as a model in preparing your own move-in letter.

We recommend that you make a copy of each tenant's move-in letter for yourself and ask him to sign the last page, indicating that he has read it.

Be sure to update the move-in letter from time to time as necessary.

C. Cash Rent and Security Deposit Checks

Every landlord's nightmare is a new tenant whose first rent or deposit check bounces and who must be dislodged with time-consuming and expensive legal proceedings.

To avoid this, never sign a rental agreement, or let a tenant move furniture into your property or take a key until you have the tenant's cash, certified check or money order for the first month's rent and security deposit. An alternative is to cash the tenant's check at the bank before the move-in date. (While you have the tenant's first check, photocopy it for your records. The information on it can be helpful if you ever need to sue to collect a judgment from the tenant.) Be sure to give the tenant a signed receipt for the deposit.

Clause 5 of the form lease and rental agreements in Chapter 2 requires tenants to pay rent on the first day of each month. If the move-in date is other than the first day of the month, rent is prorated between that day and the end of that month.

D. Organize Your Tenant Records

A good system to record all significant tenant complaints and repair requests will provide a valuable paper trail should disputes develop later—for example, regarding your right to enter a tenant's unit to make repairs, or the time it took for you to fix a problem. Without good records, the outcome of a dispute may come down to your word against your tenant's— always a precarious situation.

Set up a file folder on each property with individual files for each tenant. Include the following documents:

- rental application, references and credit and background information, including information about any cosigners
- a signed lease or rental agreement, plus any changes made along the way
- Landlord-Tenant Checklist and photos or video made at move-in, and
- signed move-in letter.

After a tenant moves in, add these documents to the individual's file:

- your written requests for entry
- rent increase notices
- records of repair requests, and details of how and when they were handled. If you keep repair records on the computer, you should regularly print out and save files from past months; if you have a master system to record all requests and complaints in one log, you would save that log separately, not necessarily put it in every tenant's file
- safety and maintenance updates and inspection reports, and
- correspondence and other relevant information.

Your computer can also be a valuable tool to keep track of tenants. Set up a simple database for each tenant with spaces for the following information:

- address or unit number
- move-in date
- home phone number
- name, address and phone number of employer
- credit information, including up-to-date information as to where tenant banks
- monthly rent amount and rent due date
- amount and purpose of deposits plus any information your state requires on location of deposit and interest payments
- vehicle make, model, color, year and license plate number
- emergency contacts, and whatever else is important to you.

Once you enter the information into your database, you can sort the list by address or other variables and easily print labels for rent increases or other notices.

If you own many rental properties, you should check into commercial computer programs that allow you to keep track of every aspect of your business, from the tracking of rents to the follow-up on repair requests. ■

Changing or Ending a Tenancy

Sometime after you've signed a lease or rental agreement you may want to make changes—perhaps you need to increase the rent or you agree to let the tenant bring in a roommate or keep a small pet. This chapter shows how to modify a signed lease or rental agreement. It also discusses how you— or your tenant—may end a tenancy, and offers tips on how to take steps to try and avoid problems, such as a tenant giving inadequate notice and breaking the lease. This chapter also summarizes basic rules for returning security deposits when a tenant leaves.

- *Writing clear lease and rental agreement provisions on notice required to end a tenancy: Chapter 2*
- *How to advertise and rent property before a current tenant leaves: Chapter 3*
- *Highlighting notice requirements in a move-in letter to the tenant: Chapter 4.*

A. How to Modify Signed Rental Agreements and Leases

All amendments to your lease or rental agreement should be in writing and signed by both you and the tenant. (Oral changes to oral agreements may be legal, but are a terrible idea.)

If you use a fixed-term lease, you cannot unilaterally alter the terms of the tenancy. For the most part, the lease fixes the terms of the ten-

ancy for the length of the lease. You can't raise the rent or change the terms of the lease until the end of the lease period unless the lease allows it or the tenant agrees. If the tenant agrees to changes, however, simply follow the directions below for amending the rental agreement.

1. Amending a Month-to-Month Rental Agreement

If you want to change one or more clauses in a month-to-month rental agreement, there is no legal requirement that you get the tenant's consent. Legally, you need simply to send the tenant a notice of the change.

Most states require 30 days' advance notice (subject to any rent control ordinances) to change a month-to-month tenancy—for example, to increase the rent. See the 50-State Law Browser for a list of your state's notice requirements, and Clause 4 of the rental agreement in Chapter 2. You'll need to consult your state statutes for the specific information on how you must deliver a 30-day notice to the tenant. (Most allow you to use first-class mail.)

 Contact the tenant and explain the changes.
It makes good personal and business sense for you or your manager to contact the tenant personally and tell him about a rent increase or other changes before you follow up with a written notice. If the tenant is opposed to your proposal,

*your personal efforts will allow you to explain
your reasons.*

You don't generally need to redo the rental
agreement in order to make a change or two.
Just keep a copy of the change with the rental
agreement. In some cases, however, you may
want the tenant to sign a new rental agreement—for example, if the tenant initiates a
change. If the change is small and simply alters
part of an existing clause—such as increasing
the rent or making the rent payable every 14
days instead of every 30 days—you can cross
out the old language, write in the new and sign
in the margin next to the new words. Make
sure the tenant also signs next to the change. Be
sure to add the date, in case there is a dispute
later as to when the change became effective.

If you do not want to rewrite the entire rental agreement, you can simply add another
page, called an "Amendment," to the original
document. The amendment should clearly re-
fer to the agreement it's changing and be
signed by the same people who signed the
original agreement. See the sample, below,
which concerns parking and pets.

2. Preparing a New Lease or Rental Agreement

If you're adding a clause, or making several
changes to your rental agreement, you will
probably find it easiest to substitute a whole
new agreement for the old one. This is easy to
do using LeaseWriter. If you prepare an entire
new agreement, be sure that you and the tenant
write "Canceled by mutual consent, effective

(date)" on the old one, and sign it. In order to
avoid the possibility of two inconsistent agreements operating at the same time, be sure that
there is no time overlap between the old and
new agreements. Similarly, so that the tenant is
always subject to a written agreement, do not
allow any gap between the cancellation date of
the old agreement and the effective date of the
new one.

 A new tenant should mean a new agreement.
*Even if a new tenant is filling out the rest of a
former tenant's lease term under the same conditions, it is never wise to allow her to operate under
the same lease or rental agreement. Start over and
prepare a new agreement in the new tenant's
name. (See Clause 10 of the form agreements in
Chapter 2.)*

B. Ending a Month-to-Month Tenancy

This section discusses a landlord's and a
tenant's responsibilities to end a month-to-
month tenancy.

1. Giving Notice to the Tenant

If you want a tenant to leave, you can end a
month-to-month tenancy simply by giving the
proper amount of notice. You don't usually
have to state a reason unless state or local law
requires it. In most places, all you need to do is

Amendment to Lease or Rental Agreement

This is an Amendment to the lease or rental agreement dated ___March 1,_____ ,

199_X_ (the "Agreement") between ___Olivia Matthew_____ ("Landlord")

and ___Steve Phillips_____ ("Tenant") regarding property

located at _1578 Maple St., Seattle_____

_____ ("the premises").

Landlord and Tenant agree to the following changes and/or additions to the Agreement:

1. Beginning on June 1, 199X, Tenant shall rent a one-car garage, adjacent to the main

   premises, from Landlord for the sum of $75 per month.

2. Tenant may keep one German shepherd dog on the premises. The dog shall be kept on a

   leash in the yard unless tenant is present. Tenant shall clean up all animal waste from

   the yard on a daily basis. Tenant agrees to repair any damages to the yard or premises

   caused by his dog, at Tenant's expense.

_____

_____

_____

_____

_____

_May 20, 199X_____ *Olivia Matthew, Landlord*_____

Date   Landlord/Landlord's Agent

_May 20, 199X_____ *Steve Phillips, Tenant*_____

Date   Tenant

_____ _____

Date   Tenant

_____ _____

Date   Tenant

give the tenant a simple written notice that complies with your state's minimum notice requirement and states the date on which the tenancy will end. After that date, the tenant no longer has the legal right to occupy the premises.

In most states, and for most rentals, a landlord who wants to terminate a month-to-month tenancy must provide the same amount of notice as a tenant—typically 30 days. (See Section 2, below.) But this is not true everywhere. For example, in Georgia, landlords must give 60 days' notice to terminate a month-to-month tenancy, while tenants need only give 30 days' notice. (See the 50-State Law Browser for a list of your state's notice requirements.) State and local rent control laws can also impose notice requirements on landlords. Things are different if you want a tenant to move because he or she has violated a material term of the rental agreement—for example, by failing to pay rent. If so, notice requirements are commonly greatly shortened, sometimes to as little as three days.

Each state (and even some cities) has its own very detailed rules and procedures for preparing and serving termination notices, and it is impossible for this book to provide all specific forms and instructions. Consult a landlords' association or local rent control board and your state statutes for information and sample forms. Once you understand how much notice you must give, how the notice must be delivered and any other requirements, you'll be in good shape to handle this work yourself—usually with no lawyer needed.

2. How Much Notice the Tenant Must Give

In most states, the tenant who decides to move out must give you at least 30 days' notice. Some states allow less than 30 days' notice in certain situations—for example, because a tenant must leave early because of military orders or health problems. And in some states, tenants who pay rent more frequently than once a month can give notice to terminate that matches their rent payment interval—for example, tenants who pay rent every two weeks would have to give 14 days' notice.

To educate your tenants as to what they can expect, make sure your rental agreement includes your state's notice requirements for ending a tenancy. (See Clause 4 of the form agreements in Chapter 2.) It is also wise to list termination notice requirements in the move-in letter you send to new tenants. (See Chapter 4, Section B.)

For details on your state's notice requirements, see the 50-State Law Browser.

Restrictions to Ending a Tenancy

The general rules for terminating a tenancy described in this chapter often don't apply in the following situations:

- **Rent control ordinances.** Many rent control cities require "just cause" (a good reason) to end a tenancy, which typically includes moving in a close relative and refurbishing the unit. You will likely have to state your legal reason in the termination notice you give the tenant.

- **Discrimination.** It is illegal to end a tenancy because of a tenant's race, religion, sex, because they have children or for any other reason constituting illegal discrimination. (Chapter 3, Section E, discusses anti-discrimination laws.)

- **Retaliation.** You can not legally terminate a tenancy to retaliate against a tenant for exercising any right under the law, such as the tenant's right to complain to governmental authorities about defective housing conditions or, in many states, to withhold rent because of a health or safety problem the landlord has failed to correct. Chapter 16 of *Every Landlord's Legal Guide*, by Marcia Stewart, Ralph Warner and Janet Portman (Nolo Press), covers how to avoid tenant retaliation claims.

3. You Should Insist on a Tenant's Written Notice of Intent to Move

In many states, a tenant's notice must be in writing and give the exact date the tenant plans to move out. Even if it is not required by law, it's a good idea to insist that the tenant give you notice in writing (as does Clause 4 of the form agreements in Chapter 2). Why bother, especially if the tenant politely calls you to say she will be out on a particular date?

Insisting on written notice will prove essential should the tenant not move as planned after you have signed a lease or rental agreement with a new tenant. Not only will this be true if, at the last minute, the tenant tries to claim that he didn't really set a firm move-out date, but it will also be invaluable if a new tenant sues you to recover the costs of temporary housing or storage fees for her belongings because you could not deliver possession of the unit. In turn, you will want to sue the old (holdover) tenant for causing the problem by failing to move out. Should this be necessary, you will have a much stronger case against the holdover tenant if you can produce a written promise to move on a specific date instead of your version of a conversation (which will undoubtedly be disputed by the tenant).

A sample Tenant's Notice of Intent to Move Out form is shown below. Give a copy of this form to any tenant who tells you he or she plans to move.

LeaseWriter includes the Tenant's Notice of Intent to Move Out form, and a filled-in sample is shown below.

LeaseWriter includes a Move-Out Letter, and a filled-in sample is shown below.

Preparing a Move-Out Letter

Chapter 4 explains how a move-in letter can help get a tenancy off to a good start. Similarly, a move-out letter can also help reduce the possibility of disputes, especially over the return of security deposits. Send the letter as soon as you receive notice of the tenant's intent to leave. Your move-out letter should explain the following to the tenant:

- how you expect the rental unit to be left, including specific cleaning requirements
- details on your final inspection procedures and how you will determine what cleaning and damage repair is necessary, requiring a deduction from the tenant's security deposit. (We recommend you check each item on the Landlord/Tenant Checklist described in Chapter 4 and also photograph or videotape the unit when the tenant leaves.)
- what kinds of deposit deductions you may legally make, and
- when and how you will send any refund that is due.

4. Accepting Rent After a 30-Day Notice Is Given

If you accept rent for any period beyond the date the tenant told you he is moving out, this likely cancels the termination notice and creates a new tenancy. An exception would be where a tenant pays you past due rent and you document this in writing.

Suppose after giving notice, the tenant asks for a little more time in which to move out. Assuming no new tenant is moving in and you are willing to accommodate this request, prepare a written agreement setting out what you have agreed to in detail and have the tenant sign it. See the sample letter, below, extending the tenant's move-out date.

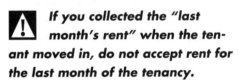 **If you collected the "last month's rent" when the tenant moved in, do not accept rent for the last month of the tenancy.** *You are legally obligated to use this money for the last month's rent. Accepting an additional month's rent may extend the tenant's tenancy.*

Tenant's Notice of Intent to Move Out

April 3, 199X _____ (date)

Anne Sakamoto _____ (landlord/manager)

888 Mill Avenue _____ (street address)

Nashville, Tennessee 37126 _____ (city and state)

Dear __Ms. Sakamoto:_____ ,(landlord/manager)

This is to notify you that the undersigned tenant(s) __Patti and Joe Ellis__

_____

_____ will be moving from

999 Brook Lane, Apartment Number 11 _____ ,

on __May 3, 199x_____ , or

30 Days _____ from today. This provides at least

30 Days _____ written notice as required in our rental agreement.

Sincerely,

Patti Ellis
_____
Tenant

Joe Ellis
_____
Tenant

_____
Tenant

Move-Out Letter

July 5, 199X _____ (date)

Jane Wasserman _____ (tenant)

123 North Street, Apartment #23 _____ (street address)

Atlanta, Georgia 30360 _____ (city and state)

Dear ___Jane_____ ,(tenant)

We hope you have enjoyed living here. In order that we may mutually end our relationship on a positive note, this move-out letter describes how we expect your unit to be left and what our procedures are for returning your security deposit.

Basically, we expect you to leave your rental unit in the same condition it was when you moved in, except for normal wear and tear. To refresh your memory on the condition of the unit when you moved in, I've attached a copy of the Landlord/Tenant Checklist you signed at the beginning of your tenancy. I'll be using this same form to inspect your unit when you leave.

Specifically, here's a list of items you should thoroughly clean before vacating:

- [ ] Floors
    - [ ] sweep wood floors
    - [ ] vacuum carpets and rugs (shampoo if necessary)
    - [ ] mop kitchen and bathroom floors
- [ ] Walls, baseboards, ceilings and built-in shelves
- [ ] Kitchen cabinets, countertops and sink, stove and oven—inside and out
- [ ] Refrigerator—clean inside and out, empty it of food, and turn it off
- [ ] Bathtubs, showers, toilets and plumbing fixtures
- [ ] Doors, windows and window coverings
- [ ] Other _____

_____

_____

_____

_____

_____

_____

_____

_____

If you have any questions as to the type of cleaning we expect, please let me know.

Please don't leave anything behind—that includes bags of garbage, clothes, food, newspapers, furniture, appliances, dishes, plants, cleaning supplies or other items that belong to you.

Please be sure you have disconnected phone and utility services, canceled all newspaper subscriptions and sent the post office a change-of-address form.

Once you have cleaned your unit and removed *all* your belongings, please call me at _____555-1234_____ to arrange for a walk-through inspection and to return all keys. Please be prepared to give me your forwarding address where we may mail your security deposit.

It's our policy to return all deposits either in person or at an address you provide within _____one month_____ after you move out. If any deductions are made—for past due rent or because the unit is damaged or not sufficiently clean—they will be explained in writing.

If you have any questions, please contact me at _____555-1234_____.

Sincerely,

Denise Parsons
_____
Landlord/Manager

5. When the Tenant Doesn't Give the Required Notice

All too often, a tenant will send or give you a "too short" notice of intent to move. And it's not unheard of for a tenant to move out with no notice or with a wave as he tosses the keys on your doorstep.

A tenant who leaves without giving enough notice has lost the right to occupy the premises, but is still obligated to pay rent through the end of the required notice period. For example, if the notice period is 30 days, but the tenant moves out after telling you 20 days ago that he intended to move, he still owes you rent for the remaining ten days.

In most states, you have a legal duty to try to re-rent the property before you can charge the tenant for giving you too little notice, but few courts expect a landlord to accomplish this in less than a month. (This rule, called the landlord's duty to mitigate damages, is discussed in Section C4, below.) You can also use the security deposit to cover unpaid rent, as discussed in Section D1, below.

6. When You or Your Tenant Violates the Rental Agreement

If you seriously violate the rental agreement and fail to fulfill your legal responsibilities—for example, by not correcting serious health or safety problems—a tenant may be able to legally move out with no written notice or by

giving less notice than is otherwise required. Called a "constructive eviction," this doctrine typically applies only when living conditions are intolerable—for example, if the tenant has had no heat for an extended period in the winter, or if a tenant's use and enjoyment of the property has been substantially impaired because of drug dealing in the building.

What exactly constitutes a constructive eviction varies slightly under the laws of different states. Generally, if you are on notice that a rental unit has serious habitability problems for an extended time, the tenant is entitled to move out on short notice or, in extreme cases, without giving notice.

Along the same lines, a landlord may evict a tenant who violates a lease or rental agreement. For example, you may give a "notice to quit" to a tenant who fails to pay rent or damages the premises, with less notice than is normally required to end a tenancy (typically three to five days, rather than 30 days). And in the case of drug dealing, many states provide for expedited eviction procedures. Because of the wide state-by-state variations on eviction rules and procedures, the details of how to evict a tenant are beyond the scope of this book.

C. How Fixed-Term Leases End

A lease lasts for a fixed term, typically one year. As a general rule, neither you nor the tenant may unilaterally terminate the tenancy or change a material condition during the period

Sample Letter Extending Tenant's Move-Out Date

June 20, 199X

Hannah Lewis
777 Broadway Terrace, Apartment #3
Richmond, Virginia 23233

Dear Hannah:

On June 1, you gave me a 30-day notice of your intent to move out on July 1. You have since requested to extend your move-out to July 18 because of last-minute problems with closing escrow on your new house. This letter is to verify our understanding that you will move out on July 18, instead of July 1, and that you will pay prorated rent for 18 days (July 1 through July 18). Prorated rent for 18 days, based on your monthly rent of $900 or $30 per day, is $540.

Please sign below to indicate your agreement to these terms.

Sincerely,

Fran Moore, Landlord

Agreed to by Hannah Lewis, Tenant:

Signature _____ *Hannah Lewis* _____

Date _____ *June 20, 199X* _____

of the lease, unless the other party has violated the terms of the lease.

If you and the tenant both live up to your promises, the lease simply ends of its own accord at the end of the lease term, and the tenant moves out. Alternatively, you may sign a new lease, with the same or different terms. As every landlord knows, however, life is not always so simple. Sooner or later, a tenant will stay beyond the end of the term without signing a new lease, or leave before it ends without any legal right to do so.

1. Giving Notice to the Tenant

Because a lease clearly states when it will expire, you may not think it's necessary to remind the tenants of the expiration date. But doing so is a very good practice, and some states or cities (especially those with rent control) actually require it.

We suggest giving the tenant at least 60 days' written notice that the lease is going to expire. This reminder has several advantages:

- **Getting the tenant out on time.** Two months' notice allows plenty of time for the tenant to look for another place if he doesn't—or you don't—want to renew the lease.
- **Giving you time to renegotiate the lease.** If you would like to continue renting to your present tenant but also want to change some lease terms or increase the rent, your notice serves to remind the tenant that the terms of the old lease will not automatically continue. Encourage the tenant to stay, but men-

tion that you need to make some changes to the lease.

- **Getting a new tenant in quickly.** If you know a tenant is going to move, you can show the unit to prospective tenants ahead of time and minimize the time the space is vacant. You must still respect the current tenant's privacy. (Chapter 3, Section B, discusses showing the unit to prospective tenants.)

 Your options may be limited in a rent control area.

If your property is subject to rent control, you may be limited in your ability to end your relationship with a current tenant. Many ordinances require "just cause" for refusing to renew a lease, which generally means that only certain reasons (such as the tenant's failure to pay rent, or your desire to move in a close relative) justify non-renewal. If your city requires "just cause," and if your decision not to renew does not meet the city's test, you may end up with a perpetual month-to-month tenant. Check your city's rent control ordinance carefully.

2. If the Tenant Remains After the Lease Expires

It's fairly common for a tenant to remain in a unit even though the lease has run out. If this happens, you have a choice: You can continue renting to the tenant, or you can take legal steps to get the tenant out.

If a tenant stays beyond the end of the lease, and you accept rent money without signing a new lease, in most states you will have created a new, month-to-month tenancy on the same terms as applied for the old lease. In a few states, you may create a new lease for the same term—such as one year. In other words, you'll be stuck with the terms and rent in the old lease, at least for the first 30 days and possibly longer. If you want to change the terms in a new lease, you must abide by the law regarding giving notice for a month-to-month tenancy (see Section B, above). It will usually take you at least a month, while you go about giving notice to your now month-to-month tenant.

To avoid problems of tenants staying longer than you want, be sure to notify the tenant that you expect him to leave at the lease expiration date and don't accept rent after this date. If a tenant just wants to stay an extra few days after a lease expires, and you agree, it is wise to put your understanding on this arrangement in a letter. (See the sample letter extending the tenant's move-out date in Section A, above.)

3. If the Tenant Leaves Early

A tenant who leaves (with or without notifying you beforehand) before a fixed-term lease expires and refuses to pay the remainder of the rent due under the lease is said to have "broken the lease." Once the tenant leaves for good, you have the legal right to take possession of the premises and re-rent to another tenant.

A key question that arises is how much does a tenant with a lease owe if she walks out early? Let's start with the general legal rule. A tenant

who signs a lease agrees at the outset to pay a fixed amount of rent: the monthly rent multiplied by the number of months of the lease. The tenant is obligated to pay this amount in monthly installments over the term of the lease. The fact that payments are made monthly doesn't change the tenant's responsibility to pay rent for the entire lease term. And the fact that a tenant who breaks a lease gives you notice of her intention to leave early changes nothing—you are still owed the money for the rest of the term. As discussed below, depending on the situation, you may use the tenant's security deposit to cover part of the shortfall, or sue the tenant for rent owed.

 Require tenants to notify you of extended absences.
Clause 16 of the form lease and rental agreements (Chapter 2) requires tenants to inform you when they will be gone for an extended time, such as two or more weeks.

By requiring tenants to notify you of long absences, you'll know whether property has been abandoned or the tenant is simply on vacation. In addition, if you have such a clause and, under its authority, enter an apparently abandoned unit only to be confronted later by an indignant tenant, you can defend yourself by pointing out that the tenant violated the lease.

4. Your Duty to Mitigate Your Loss If the Tenant Leaves Early

If a tenant breaks the lease and moves out without legal justification, you can't just sit back and wait until the end of the term of the lease, and then sue the departed tenant for the total amount of your lost rent. In most states, you must try to re-rent the property reasonably quickly and subtract the rent you receive from the amount the original tenant owed you.

Even if this isn't the legal rule in your state, trying to re-rent is obviously a sound business strategy. It's much better to have rent coming in every month than to wait, leaving a rental unit vacant for months, and then try to sue (and collect from) a tenant who may be long gone, broke or otherwise difficult to collect from.

If you don't make an attempt (or make an inadequate one) to re-rent, and instead sue the former tenant for the whole rent, you will collect only what the judge thinks is the difference between the fair rental value of the property had you re-rented it and the original tenant's promised rent. This can depend on how easy it is to re-rent in your area. Also, a judge is sure to give you some time (probably at least 30 days) to find a new tenant.

5. How to Mitigate Your Damages

When you're sure that a tenant has left permanently, then you can turn your attention to re-renting the unit.

You do not need to relax your standards for acceptable tenants—for example, you are entitled to reject applicants with poor credit or rental histories. Also, you need not give the suddenly available property priority over other rental units that you would normally attend to first.

You are not required to rent the premises at a rate substantially below its fair market value.

Keep in mind, however, that refusing to rent at less than the original rate may be foolish. If you are unable to ultimately collect from the former tenant, you will get *no* income from the property instead of less. You will have ended up hurting no one but yourself.

Keep Good Records

If you end up suing a former tenant, you will want to be able to show the judge that you acted reasonably in your attempts to re-rent the property. Don't rely on your memory and powers of persuasion to convince the judge. Keep detailed records, including:

- the original lease
- receipts for cleaning and painting, with photos of the unit showing the need for repairs, if any
- your expenses for storing or properly disposing of any belongings the tenant left
- receipts for advertising the property and bills from credit reporting agencies investigating potential renters
- a log of the time you spent showing the property, and the value of that time
- a log of any people who offered to rent and, if you rejected them, documentation as to why, and
- if the current rent is less than that the original tenant paid, a copy of the new lease.

When Leaving Early Is Justified

There are some important exceptions to the blanket rule that a tenant who breaks a lease owes you the rent for the entire lease term. A tenant who leaves early may *not* owe if:

- **Your rental unit is unsafe or otherwise uninhabitable.** If you don't live up to your obligations to provide habitable housing—for example, if you fail to maintain the unit in accordance with health and safety codes—a court will conclude that you have "constructively evicted" the tenant. That releases the tenant from further obligations under the lease. (Section B6, above, discusses constructive evictions.)

- **You have rented—or could rent—the unit to someone else.** Most courts require landlords to try to soften ("mitigate") the ex-tenant's liability for the remaining rent by attempting to find a new rent-paying tenant as soon as possible. The new tenant's rent is credited against what the former tenant owed. (Because this "mitigation of damages" rule can be so important, Section C4, above, looks at it in more detail.)

- **State law allows the tenant to leave early.** A few states have laws that list allowable reasons to break a lease.

For example, in Delaware a tenant need only give 30 days' notice to end a long-term lease if he needs to move because his present employer relocated or because health problems (of the tenant or a family member) require a permanent move. Some states, such as Georgia, allow members of the military to break a lease because of a change in military orders. If your tenant has a good reason for a sudden move, you may want to research your state's law to see whether or not he's still on the hook for rent.

- **The rental unit is damaged or destroyed.** If a tenant's home is significantly damaged—either by natural disaster or any other reason beyond his control—he has the right to consider the lease at an end and to move out. State laws vary on the extent of the landlord's responsibility depending on the cause of the damage. If a fire, flood, tornado, earthquake or other natural disaster makes the dwelling unlivable, or if a third party is the cause of the destruction (for instance, a fire due to an arsonist), your best bet is to look to your insurance policy for help in repairing or rebuilding the unit and to assist your tenants in resettlement.

6. The Tenant's Right to Find a Replacement Tenant

A tenant who wishes to leave before the lease expires may offer to find a suitable new tenant, so that the flow of rent will remain uninterrupted, and he will be off the hook for future rent payments. Unless you have a new tenant waiting, you have nothing to lose by cooperating. And refusing to cooperate could hurt you: If you refuse to accept an excellent new tenant and then withhold the lease-breaking tenant's deposit or sue for unpaid rent, you may wind up losing in court since, after all, you turned down the chance to reduce your losses (mitigate your damages).

Of course, if the rental market is really tight in your area, you may be able to lease the unit easily at a higher rent or you may already have an even better prospective tenant on your waiting list. In that case, you won't care if a tenant breaks the lease, and you may not be interested in any new tenant he provides.

If you and the outgoing tenant agree on a replacement tenant, you and the new tenant should sign a new lease.

7. When You Can Sue

If a tenant leaves prematurely, you may need to go to court and sue for your re-rental costs and the difference between the original and the replacement rent. (Obviously, you should first use the tenant's deposit, if possible, to cover these costs. See Section D, below.)

Deciding *where* to sue is usually easy: Small claims court is usually the court of choice because it's fast, affordable and doesn't require a lawyer. The only exception is in states where

small claims courts have very low dollar limits and you are owed lots more.

Knowing *when* to sue is trickier. You may be eager to start legal proceedings as soon as the original tenant leaves, but if you do, you won't know the extent of your losses because you might find another tenant who will make up part of the lost rent. Must you wait until the end of the original tenant's lease? Or can you bring suit when you re-rent the property?

The standard approach, and one that all states allow, is to go to court after you re-rent the property. At this point, your losses—your expenses and the rent differential, if any—are known and final. The disadvantage is that you have had no income from that property since the original tenant left, and the original tenant may be long gone and not, practically speaking, worth chasing down.

Nolo's Book on Small Claims Court

Everybody's Guide to Small Claims Court (National Edition), by Ralph Warner (Nolo Press), provides detailed advice on bringing or defending a small claims court case, preparing evidence and witnesses for court and collecting your court judgment when you win. (See the order form at the back of this book.) *Everybody's Guide to Small Claims Court* will also be useful in defending yourself against a tenant who sues you in small claims court—for example, claiming that you failed to return a cleaning or security deposit.

D. Returning Security Deposits When a Tenancy Ends

Most states set very specific rules for the return of security deposits when a tenant leaves—whether voluntarily or by your ending the tenancy. A landlord's failure to return security deposits as legally required can result in substantial financial penalties if a tenant files suit.

1. Basic Rules for Returning Deposits

You are generally entitled to deduct from a tenant's security deposit whatever amount you need to fix damaged or dirty property (outside of "ordinary wear and tear") or to make up unpaid rent. But you must make your deductions and return deposits correctly. While the specific rules vary from state to state, you usually have between 14 and 30 days after the tenant leaves to return the deposit. (See the 50-State Law Browser for security deposit rules in your state.)

State security deposit statutes typically require you to mail the following within the time limit to the tenant's last known address (or forwarding address if you have one):

- The tenant's entire deposit with interest if required
- A written itemized accounting of deductions, including back rent and costs of cleaning and damage repair, together with payment for any deposit balance. The statement should list each deduction and briefly explain what it's for.

Even if there is no specific time limit in your state or law requiring itemization,

promptly presenting the tenant with a written itemization of all deductions and a clear reason why each was made is an essential part of a savvy landlord's overall plan to avoid disputes with tenants. In general, we recommend three to four weeks as a reasonable time.

2. Penalties for Violating Security Deposit Laws

If you don't follow state security deposit laws to the letter, you may pay a heavy price if a tenant sues you and wins. In addition to whatever amount you wrongfully withheld, you may have to pay the tenant extra or punitive damages (penalties imposed when the judge feels that the defendant has acted especially outrageously) and court costs. In many states if you "willfully" (deliberately and not through inadvertence) violate the security deposit statute, you may forfeit your right to retain any part of the deposit and may be liable for two or three times the amount wrongfully withheld, plus attorney fees and costs.

3. If the Deposit Doesn't Cover Damage and Unpaid Rent

If the security deposit doesn't cover what a tenant owes you, you may wish to file a small claims lawsuit against the former tenant.

LeaseWriter provides forms and instructions for returning and itemizing security deposits, and filled-in samples are shown below.

Letter for Returning Entire Security Deposit

October 11, 199X
Date

Gerry Fraser
Tenant
976 Park Place
Street address
Sacramento, CA 95840
City and State

Dear_____ Gerry _____,
　　　　　　　　Tenant

Here is an itemization of your _____ $1,500 _____ security deposit on the property at

976 Park Place _____,

which you rented from me on a _____ month-to-month _____ basis on

March 1 _____,199 X _____, and vacated on _____ September 30 _____, 199 X .

As you left the rental property in satisfactory condition, I am returning the entire amount of the

security deposit of _____ $1,500, plus $150 in interest, for a total of $1,650 _____.

Sincerely,

Tom Stein
Landlord/Manager

Security Deposit Itemization
(Deductions for Repairs, Cleaning and Unpaid Rent)

Date: _December 19, 199X_

From: _Timothy Gottman_

8910 Pine Avenue

Philadelphia, Pennsylvania

To: _Monique Todd_

999 Laurel Drive

Philadelphia, Pennsylvania

Property Address: _456 Pine Avenue #7, Philadelphia, Pennsylvania_

Rental Period: _January 1, 199X, to October 31, 199X_

1. Security Deposit Received $ _1,200_

2. Interest on Deposit (if required by lease or law): $ _N/A_

3. Total Credit (sum of lines 1 and 2) $ _1,200_

4. Itemized Repairs and Related Losses:

   Carpet repair $160, drapery cleaning $140,

   plaster repair $400, painting of living room

   $100 (receipts attached)

   Total Repair Cost: $ _800_

5. Necessary Cleaning:

   Sum paid to resident manager for 10 hours

   cleaning at $20/hour: debris-filled garage,

   dirty stove and refrigerator

   Total Cleaning Cost: $ _200_

6. Defaults in Rent Not Covered by Any Court Judgment (list dates and rates):

   5 days at $20 day from November 6 to

   November 11 (date of court judgment of date

   of physical eviction) $100

   Total Rent Defaults: $ _100_

7. Amount of Court Judgment for Rent, Costs, Attorney Fees: $ _____ 1,160 _____

8. Other Deductions:

   Specify: _____

   _____

   _____ $ _____

9. Amount Owed (line 3 minus the sum of lines 4, 5, 6, 7 and 8)

   ☒ a. Total Amount Tenant Owes Landlord: $ _____ 1,060 _____

   ☐ b. Total Amount Landlord Owes Tenant: $ _____

Comments: _____ The security deposit has been applied as follows: $1,000 for damage and cleaning charges, $100 for defaults in rent (not covered by any court judgment) and the remaining $100 towards payment of the $1,160 court judgment. This leaves $1,060 still owed on the judgment. Please send that amount to me at once or I shall take appropriate legal action to collect it.

How to Find Your State Statutes Online

Many states have made their statutes available online. If your state has done so, you can use your computer and browser to read any of the statutes cited in the 50-State Law Browser.

To show you how to find landlord-tenant statutes online, we're going to assume that you have a basic familiarity with your computer, browser and the Internet. For more detailed descriptions of how to do legal research online, see *Legal Research: Online and in the Library,* by Stephen Elias and Susan Levinkind (Nolo Press).

Let's suppose that you are a landlord in Missouri and would like to read your state's statute on security deposits. After consulting the 50-State Law Browser, you know that the security deposit statute is Section 535.300. The following steps show you how to find that statute.

Figure 1

Step 1: Go to Findlaw. We suggest that you use the Internet search engine known as Findlaw (www.findlaw.com). When you enter Findlaw's URL in your browser, you'll see their Homepage, as shown in Figure 1.

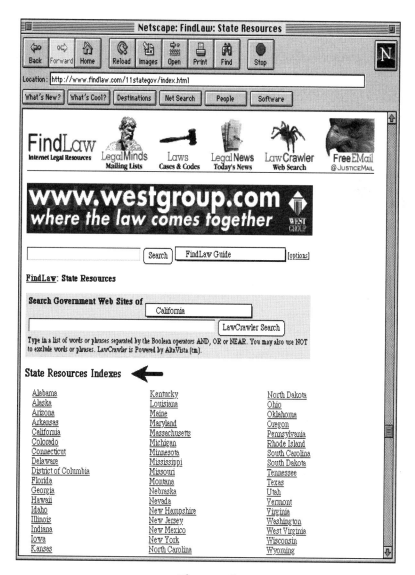

Figure 2

Step 2: Choose the link that will take you to state statutes.

In Figure 1, you see a number of links. Since you're looking for state statutes, you'll want to click on the State Laws link, under the Laws: Cases & Codes main link. The resulting page is shown in Figure 2.

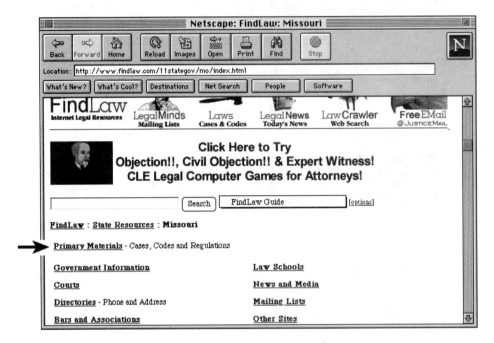

Figure 3

Step 3: Choose your state. As you look at the page shown in Figure 2 (you may have to scroll down a bit), you'll see the 50 states listed under State Resources Indexes. When you click on the state you're interested in—for this example, Missouri—you'll see the page shown in Figure 3.

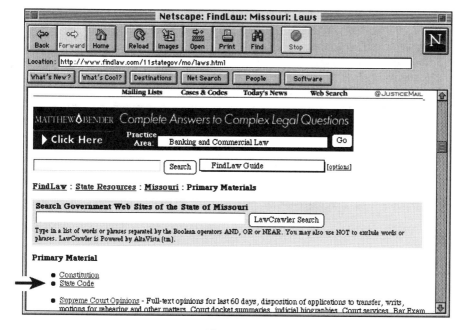

Figure 4

Step 4: Choose the link that will take you to the state statutes.

In Figure 3, you'll see that Findlaw has put Missouri cases, codes and regulations under its Primary Materials link. (Remember, "codes" is another word for statutes.) When you choose that link, you'll get the screen shown in Figure 4.

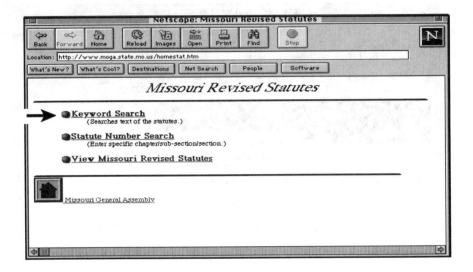

Figure 5

Step 5: Choose the State Code. Under the Primary Materials link, you could choose to go to the Constitution or the Code. When you click on the State Code link, you'll get the page shown in Figure 5.

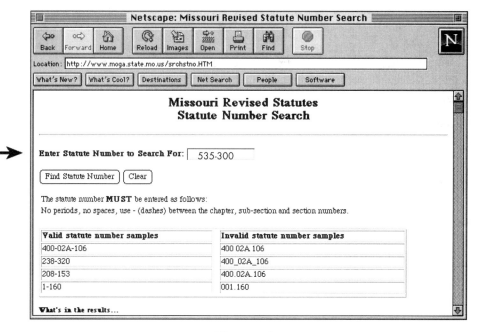

Figure 6

Step 6: Search for your statute. You'll see that the Missouri site gives you three ways to read the statutes:

1. If you don't know the statute's number, you can enter a "keyword" that is likely to be in it. For example, you could ask Findlaw to look for statutes containing the words "security" and "deposit."
2. If you know the statute number, you could ask Findlaw to take you directly there.
3. If you just want to browse through the statutes, you could ask Findlaw to give you the code's table of contents, which is linked to the codes.

For our example, we'll ask Findlaw to do the number search described in 2, above. Clicking on the Statute Number Search link brings us to a page with a query box, shown in Figure 6.

When you do a search like this for your state, you may find that your state's statute page is designed differently than the one shown in Figure 5. But the basic choice of initial "clicks" in Findlaw is the same for every state. Usually, you can figure out how to get to the codes with a little trial and error.

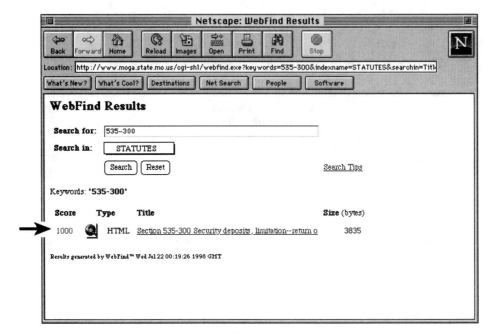

Figure 7

Step 7: Type in the statute number. When you enter the statute number, as directed in the page's instructions, you'll be taken to another page with a link to the statute, shown in Figure 7.

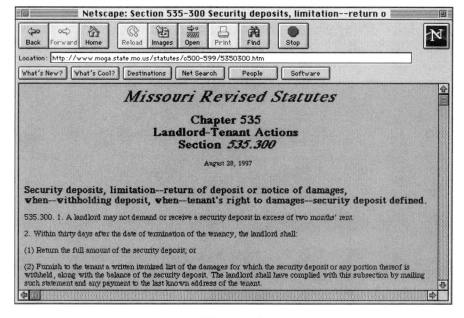

Figure 8

Step 8: Ask for the statute. Finally, you're close to the statute itself. Clicking on the Section 535-300 link brings you to the page shown in Figure 8.

User's Guide

Users' Guide

Leases and Rental Agreements

Index

CATALOG

...more from Nolo Press

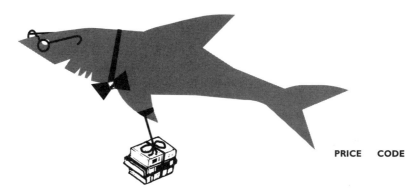

		PRICE	CODE

BUSINESS

	Title	Price	Code
	The California Nonprofit Corporation Handbook	$29.95	NON
	The California Professional Corporation Handbook	$34.95	PROF
	The Employer's Legal Handbook	$29.95	EMPL
☐	Form Your Own Limited Liability Company (Book w/Disk—PC)	$34.95	LIAB
☐	Hiring Independent Contractors: The Employer's Legal Guide, (Book w/Disk—PC)	$29.95	HICI
☐	How to Form a CA Nonprofit Corp.—w/Corp. Records Binder & PC Disk	$49.95	CNP
☐	How to Form a Nonprofit Corp., Book w/Disk (PC)—National Edition	$39.95	NNP
☐	How to Form Your Own Calif. Corp.—w/Corp. Records Binder & Disk—PC	$39.95	CACI
☐	How to Form Your Own California Corporation (Book w/Disk—PC)	$34.95	CCOR
☐	How to Form Your Own Florida Corporation, (Book w/Disk—PC)	$39.95	FLCO
☐	How to Form Your Own New York Corporation, (Book w/Disk—PC)	$39.95	NYCO
☐	How to Form Your Own Texas Corporation, (Book w/Disk—PC)	$39.95	TCOR
	How to Mediate Your Dispute	$18.95	MEDI
	How to Write a Business Plan	$21.95	SBS

☐ Book with disk
◉ Book with CD-ROM

	PRICE	CODE
The Independent Paralegal's Handbook	$29.95	PARA
Legal Guide for Starting & Running a Small Business, Vol. 1	$24.95	RUNS
💾 Legal Guide for Starting & Running a Small Business, Vol. 2: Legal Forms	$29.95	RUNS2
Marketing Without Advertising	$19.00	MWAD
💾 The Partnership Book: How to Write a Partnership Agreement, (Book w/Disk—PC)	$34.95	PART
Sexual Harassment on the Job	$18.95	HARS
Starting and Running a Successful Newsletter or Magazine	$24.95	MAG
Take Charge of Your Workers' Compensation Claim (California Edition)	$29.95	WORK
Tax Savvy for Small Business	$28.95	SAVVY
Trademark: Legal Care for Your Business and Product Name	$29.95	TRD
Wage Slave No More: Law & Taxes for the Self-Employed	$24.95	WAGE
Your Rights in the Workplace	$21.95	YRW

CONSUMER

	PRICE	CODE
Fed Up With the Legal System: What's Wrong & How to Fix It	$9.95	LEG
How to Win Your Personal Injury Claim	$24.95	PICL
Nolo's Everyday Law Book	$21.95	EVL
Nolo's Pocket Guide to California Law	$11.95	CLAW
Trouble-Free Travel...And What to Do When Things Go Wrong	$14.95	TRAV

ESTATE PLANNING & PROBATE

	PRICE	CODE
8 Ways to Avoid Probate (Quick & Legal Series)	$15.95	PRO8
How to Probate an Estate (California Edition)	$34.95	PAE
Make Your Own Living Trust	$24.95	LITR
Nolo's Law Form Kit: Wills	$14.95	KWL
💾 Nolo's Will Book, (Book w/Disk—PC)	$29.95	SWIL
Plan Your Estate	$24.95	NEST
The Quick and Legal Will Book	$15.95	QUIC

💾 Book with disk

◉ Book with CD-ROM

		PRICE	CODE

FAMILY MATTERS

	PRICE	CODE
Child Custody: Building Parenting Agreements that Work	$24.95	CUST
Divorce & Money: How to Make the Best Financial Decisions During Divorce	$26.95	DIMO
Do Your Own Divorce in Oregon	$19.95	ODIV
Get a Life: You Don't Need a Million to Retire Well	$18.95	LIFE
The Guardianship Book (California Edition)	$24.95	GB
How to Adopt Your Stepchild in California	$22.95	ADOP
How to Change Child Support in California (Quick & Legal Series)	$19.95	CHLD
A Legal Guide for Lesbian and Gay Couples	$24.95	LG
The Living Together Kit	$24.95	LTK
Nolo's Pocket Guide to Family Law	$14.95	FLD

GOING TO COURT

	PRICE	CODE
Collect Your Court Judgment (California Edition)	$24.95	JUDG
The Criminal Law Handbook: Know Your Rights, Survive the System	$24.95	KYR
How to Seal Your Juvenile & Criminal Records (California Edition)	$24.95	CRIM
How to Sue For Up to 25,000...and Win!	$29.95	MUNI
Everybody's Guide to Small Claims Court in California	$18.95	CSCC
Everybody's Guide to Small Claims Court (National Edition)	$18.95	NSCC
Fight Your Ticket ... and Win! (California Edition)	$19.95	FYT
How to Change Your Name in California	$29.95	NAME
Mad at Your Lawyer	$21.95	MAD
Represent Yourself in Court: How to Prepare & Try a Winning Case	$29.95	RYC

HOMEOWNERS, LANDLORDS & TENANTS

	PRICE	CODE
The Deeds Book (California Edition)	$16.95	DEED
Dog Law	$14.95	DOG
▣ Every Landlord's Legal Guide (National Edition, Book w/Disk—PC)	$34.95	ELLI
Every Tenant's Legal Guide	$24.95	EVTEN
For Sale by Owner in California	$24.95	FSBO
How to Buy a House in California	$24.95	BHCA

▣ Book with disk

⦿ Book with CD-ROM

	PRICE	CODE
The Landlord's Law Book, Vol. 1: Rights & Responsibilities (California Edition)	$34.95	LBRT
The Landlord's Law Book, Vol. 2: Evictions (California Edition)	$34.95	LBEV
Leases & Rental Agreements (Quick & Legal Series)	$18.95	LEAR
Neighbor Law: Fences, Trees, Boundaries & Noise	$17.95	NEI
Stop Foreclosure Now in California	$29.95	CLOS
Tenants' Rights (California Edition)	$19.95	CTEN

HUMOR

29 Reasons Not to Go to Law School	$9.95	29R
Poetic Justice	$9.95	PJ

IMMIGRATION

How to Get a Green Card: Legal Ways to Stay in the U.S.A.	$24.95	GRN
U.S. Immigration Made Easy	$39.95	IMEZ

MONEY MATTERS

▣ 101 Law Forms for Personal Use: (Quick and Legal Series, Book w/disk—PC)	$24.95	101LAW
Chapter 13 Bankruptcy: Repay Your Debts	$29.95	CH13
Credit Repair (Quick & Legal Series)	$15.95	CREP
▣ The Financial Power of Attorney Workbook (Book w/disk—PC)	$24.95	FINPOA
How to File for Bankruptcy	$26.95	HFB
Money Troubles: Legal Strategies to Cope With Your Debts	$19.95	MT
Nolo's Law Form Kit: Personal Bankruptcy	$14.95	KBNK
Stand Up to the IRS	$24.95	SIRS
Take Control of Your Student Loans	$19.95	SLOAN

PATENTS AND COPYRIGHTS

▣ The Copyright Handbook: How to Protect and Use Written Works (Book w/disk—PC)	$29.95	COHA
Copyright Your Software	$39.95	CYS

▣ Book with disk

◉ Book with CD-ROM

	PRICE	CODE
The Inventor's Notebook	$19.95	INOT
▣ License Your Invention (Book w/Disk—PC)	$39.95	LICE
The Patent Drawing Book	$29.95	DRAW
Patent, Copyright & Trademark	$24.95	PCTM
Patent It Yourself	$44.95	PAT
Software Development: A Legal Guide (Book with CD-ROM)	$44.95	SFT

RESEARCH & REFERENCE

	PRICE	CODE
Government on the Net, (Book w/CD-ROM—Windows/Macintosh)	$39.95	GONE
Law on the Net, (Book w/CD-ROM—Windows/Macintosh)	$39.95	LAWN
Legal Research: How to Find & Understand the Law	$21.95	LRES
Legal Research Made Easy (Video)	$89.95	LRME

SENIORS

	PRICE	CODE
Beat the Nursing Home Trap	$18.95	ELD
The Conservatorship Book (California Edition)	$29.95	CNSV
Social Security, Medicare & Pensions	$19.95	SOA

SOFTWARE

Call or check our website for special discounts on Software!

	PRICE	CODE
California Incorporator 2.0—DOS	$79.95	INCI
Living Trust Maker CD—Windows/Macintosh	$79.95	LTM2
Small Business Legal Pro 3 CD—Windows/Macintosh CD-ROM	$79.95	SBCD3
Nolo's Partnership Maker 1.0—DOS	$79.95	PAGI1
Personal RecordKeeper 4.0 CD—Windows/Macintosh	$49.95	RKM4
Patent It Yourself CD—Windows	$229.95	PYP12
WillMaker 6.0—Windows/Macintosh CD-ROM	$69.95	WD6

▣ Book with disk

⊙ Book with CD-ROM

Special Upgrade Offer
Get 25% off the latest edition off your Nolo book

It's important to have the most current legal information. Because laws and legal procedures change often, we update our books regularly. To help keep you up-to-date we are extending this special upgrade offer. Cut out and mail the title portion of the cover of your old Nolo book and we'll give you 25% off the retail price of the NEW EDITION of that book when you purchase directly from us. For more information call us at 1-800-992-6656. This offer is to individuals only.

ORDER FORM

Code	Quantity	Title	Unit price	Total
		Subtotal		
		California residents add Sales Tax		
		Basic Shipping ($6.50)		
		UPS RUSH delivery $8.00–any size order*		
		TOTAL		

Name

Address

(UPS to street address, Priority Mail to P.O. boxes)

* Delivered in 3 business days from receipt of S.F. Bay Area use regular shipping. order.

FOR FASTER SERVICE, USE YOUR CREDIT CARD & OUR TOLL-FREE NUMBERS

Order 24 hours a day	1-800-992-6656
Fax your order	1-800-645-0895
Online	www.nolo.com

METHOD OF PAYMENT

☐ Check enclosed

☐ VISA ☐ MasterCard ☐ Discover Card ☐ American Express

Account #   Expiration Date

Authorizing Signature

Daytime Phone

PRICES SUBJECT TO CHANGE.

VISIT OUR STORES   VISIT US ONLINE

You'll find our complete line of books and software, all at a discount.

BERKELEY
950 Parker Street
Berkeley, CA 94710
1-510-704-2248

SAN JOSE
111 N. Market Street, #115
San Jose, CA 95113
1-408-271-7240

on the Internet

www.nolo.com

NOLO PRESS 950 PARKER ST., BERKELEY, CA 94710

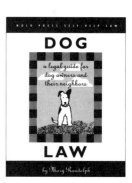

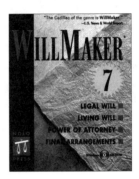